Dec 2020

Dear Casa[...]

You a such [...] er
forget that. [...] uch
a challenge but we usually have such
growth from challenges.
May the following days bring you much
joy + blessings.
I hope you enjoy this book + see
all the kindness + love Jesus
express. He was a man of action,
like you!

Merry Christmas!
Lovingly,
Cathy Samanan

STORIES
of
HEALING

Jesus and his followers

STORIES
of
HEALING
Jesus and his followers

A revised and expanded edition of
Jesus' Healings, parts 1–3
and
New Testament Healings

By

Mary Jo Beebe | Olene E. Carroll | Nancy H. Fischer

Illustrated by

Genevieve Meek

The Christian Science Publishing Society
210 Massachusetts Avenue, Boston, Massachusetts 02115 USA

The Christian Science Publishing Society
210 Massachusetts Avenue, Boston, Massachusetts 02115 USA
www.christianscience.com

First edition published as four volumes: 2002   *Jesus' Healings*, part 1; *Jesus' Healings*, part 2; *Jesus' Healings*, part 3
2003   *New Testament Healings: Peter, Paul, and Friends*

Revised and expanded edition: 2020   *Stories of Healing: Jesus and His Followers*

The colophon design is a trademark of The Christian Science Publishing Society, registered in the United States and internationally.

ISBN: 978-0-87510-527-7
G500B52642EN

Printed in the United States of America

25 24 23 22 21 20 1 2 3 4 5

TABLE *of* CONTENTS

LEARN MORE HERE

SOURCES AND INDEX

INTRODUCTION

As the Son of God, Jesus was the best spiritual healer who ever lived. He taught people how to live happy, helpful, healthy lives. You can learn about Jesus in the Bible—especially in the books of Matthew, Mark, Luke, and John. These books are called the Gospels. The word "gospel" means good news, and Jesus showed us the good news that God's love helps and heals us!

Jesus spent his life helping people. He was kind to everyone, including those who were most left out. One of the most important ways Jesus showed his love for people was by healing them. Everywhere he went, he healed all types of people, curing whatever problems they had.

This book, *Stories of Healing: Jesus and His Followers*, tells about the times recorded in the Gospels when Jesus healed. And it tells about the times in the book of Acts when several of Jesus' followers cured people. There's a testimony section, too, where children and adults from today share how they've been healed by learning more about God. All of these healings—the ones from the Bible and from today—are true stories.

Stories of Healing also explains the spiritual truths behind these healings. Mary Baker Eddy, who started the Church of Christ, Scientist, learned these truths from God as she studied the Bible, especially Jesus' healings. She wrote down all she discovered in *Science and Health with Key to the Scriptures*. Here are a few important ideas from *Science and Health*:

• God, divine Spirit, is all-powerful and entirely good.

• God is the only creator, and creation is spiritual and complete—perfect in every way.

• As God's children, we are spiritual, made in God's image and likeness.

Jesus understood these ideas. He wasn't tricked into believing that anyone could be sick or mean or poor or sad because he knew that God's children are always pure and good. Jesus' thinking was filled with truths from God, with the understanding that God is everywhere and all-powerful. In fact, Jesus' thoughts were so close to God that he saw people the way God sees them—as spiritual and good—and this brought healing.

Even as a little boy, Jesus felt very close to God. The Bible says that, as a child, he was "filled with wisdom: and the grace of God was upon him" (Luke 2:40). God had given Jesus important work to do—to save people from all kinds of problems and doing what was wrong (see Matthew 1:21).

The Bible describes Jesus' healings starting when he was about 30 years old. For the next three years, he helped and healed people, and taught them how to feel closer to God.

Jesus did his job perfectly. But he didn't do it through his own power. He healed through God's power. And he explained this spiritual power to others so they could learn how to heal, too.

Jesus sent his closest students out into the world to "heal the sick, cleanse the lepers, raise the dead, cast out devils" (Matthew 10:5–8). But they weren't the only ones he expected to be healers. Jesus wanted all his followers—including those who follow his example today—to heal through the same spiritual understanding he had.

You can be a healer, too—right here and right now. Jesus loved children and encouraged adults to be more like them. He even chose a child as an example of the "greatest in the kingdom of heaven" (Matthew 18:4).

The many healings in this book and the explanations about how they happened can help you be a follower of Jesus and heal the same way he did. ■

HOW *this book works*

The stories in this book are true stories. The first two sections include retellings of the healings by Jesus and his followers found in the Bible. Those healings took place about two thousand years ago. But healings are happening today, too. You can find examples of those healings in the "Healings from Today" section, starting on page 239.

When verses from the Bible are used, they are from the King James Version.

The colors and symbols throughout the book lead you to information about many of the people, places, customs, and terms in the stories. The next page explains these colors and symbols.

WORD BUBBLE ICON
When you find this symbol in the story, look for it (in the same color) in the margin to find more information about the story.

MAGNIFYING GLASS ICON
When you find this symbol in the story, look for it (in the same color) in the margin to see where else you can go in the book or in the Bible to learn more about the story.

CONCEPTS
CUSTOMS
GLOSSARY
PEOPLE
PLACES

COLOR KEY
When you find a word in a color, you can look it up in the section in the back of the book that matches the color of the word.

STAR ICON
When you find a yellow star at the end of the story, go to the page number in the star to find a healing from today that's related to the Bible story.

Jesus' HEALINGS

MAN HEALED OF MENTAL ILLNESS
— (Capernaum) —

You can find another account of this healing in Mark 1:21–28.

Jesus left his hometown of Nazareth in Galilee and traveled to Capernaum. This busy city was on the shore of a beautiful lake called the Sea of Galilee.

While in Capernaum, Jesus taught on the Sabbath day in the synagogue. That's where the Jews met to pray and learn about God.

To find more information on color-coded terms, see pages 261–282.

CONCEPTS CUSTOMS GLOSSARY PEOPLE PLACES

The people listening to Jesus were amazed at his **word**, or teaching. Jesus listened to God's thoughts, and when he taught, he spoke God's thoughts.

Jesus knew that God is good and is the only power. And he knew that everyone is created in the image and likeness of God, Spirit. When Jesus taught, the people felt the power of his words and saw that his understanding of God healed people. That didn't happen when the scribes taught them.

Mark adds that Jesus "taught them as one that had authority, and not as the scribes" (Mark 1:22).

II TIMOTHY 1:7

"For God hath not given us the spirit of fear; but of power, and of love, and of a sound mind."

Demons are not real, and Jesus wasn't tricked into thinking they were. Jesus knew that the power of God, the one Spirit, was right there in that synagogue to heal the man. So, he wasn't afraid. God, Spirit, is right here with us, too, taking away fear and giving us calm, strong thoughts.

One Sabbath when Jesus was teaching, there was a mentally ill man in the synagogue. In those days, people believed invisible beings called **demons** or evil spirits could make them sick. So the people in the synagogue thought this man had demons in him.

Suddenly, the man screamed, "Let us alone! What do you want with us, Jesus of Nazareth? I know what you're up to. You're the Holy One of God, and you've come to destroy us!" The "Holy One

of God" was another name for "**Messiah**." Many Jews believed the Messiah was a king that God would send to help and heal them.

Jesus knew that demons were just bad or wild thoughts. And he was sure that God, who is all-good and all-powerful, could destroy wild thoughts.

The sick man was out of control. No one knew what he would do next. The people were probably really scared.

But Jesus wasn't afraid. He stopped the man by shouting two strong orders: "Be quiet! Get out of him!"

Jesus knew that God is always in control and that demons, or bad thoughts, had no power over God or this man.

Right after Jesus spoke, the man fell down,

but he wasn't hurt. Jesus' strong commands had destroyed the man's belief in demons. Those wild thoughts had never been part of the man God made, so they couldn't be part of this man. He was completely healed.

Everyone was amazed. They said to each other, "What a powerful word this is! Jesus tells demons to leave, and they leave!" Jesus had shown them that the power of God—the one Spirit—destroys belief in evil.

Because of this wonderful healing, news about Jesus spread quickly around Galilee. ■

What can YOU do?

At some point, you may see someone who is out of control. It might be scary to see the person acting or speaking in a wild way, but like Jesus, you don't have to be afraid. God is always in control. That person's true nature is perfect as God's child. You can be still and calm in your thought and know that God is taking care of that person—and taking care of you, too.

LUKE 4:38–39

PETER'S MOTHER-IN-LAW HEALED OF FEVER

You can find other accounts of this healing in Matthew 8:14–15 and Mark 1:29–31.

Jesus had just healed a man with a mental illness while he was teaching in the synagogue in Capernaum. 🔍 He then went home with Peter, one of his twelve disciples. 💬

🔍 **SEE** "Man Healed of Mental Illness (Capernaum)," p. 14.

💬 Mark says that the house they went to belonged to both Peter and Andrew (see Mark 1:29). Andrew was Peter's brother and was also one of Jesus' disciples.

To find more information on color-coded terms, see pages 261–282.

CONCEPTS | CUSTOMS | GLOSSARY | PEOPLE | PLACES

Luke says this was a "great fever," which means that it was a serious illness (Luke 4:38).

Matthew says Jesus "touched her hand" (Matthew 8:15). Mark says Jesus "took her by the hand, and lifted her up" (Mark 1:31). See **Healing by Touch**, p. 267.

What can YOU do?

You might be asked to pray for someone. What if you feel you're not old enough or don't know enough? It helps to remember what Jesus knew—that God is the One who heals. And since God is always with everyone, we can all—big and little—turn to God for healing.

Jesus might have expected to have a nice meal waiting for him at the house. But when he arrived, someone in Peter's family needed help.

Peter's wife's mother was sick with a fever. Her family must have been very worried about her because the minute Jesus arrived, they begged him to help her. Jesus was ready and willing to help. He knew that God is always present and able to heal.

Jesus went to the sick woman and stood by her. He shut out the thoughts of sickness to make room for God's thoughts. That's a way of praying. Jesus knew this woman was God's child and that sickness had no power to hurt her.

He gave a strong command to the fever that was like saying, "You have no power! You are nothing! Get out of here!"

And the fever was gone!

Immediately, the woman got up and began caring for her guests. She didn't have to rest at all. She felt strong and ready to work.

Serving everyone a nice, big meal probably made her very happy. It was a great way to say thank you for her healing! ■

EPHESIANS 6:10

"Be strong in the Lord, and in the power of his might."

Jesus stood up to fear and sickness with strong thoughts and words. God makes us strong, too. Just like Jesus, we can say to any bad thoughts telling us we're sick, "No! Get out! Spirit, God, is the only power. God fills all space, so there's no place for anything unlike God." When we're sure of God's all-power, thoughts of sickness are destroyed—and we are healed.

MARK 1:40–45

MAN HEALED OF LEPROSY

You can find other accounts of this healing in Matthew 8:1–4 and Luke 5:12–15.

After healing Peter's mother-in-law, Jesus traveled all over Galilee.  He taught and healed people with many kinds of sicknesses, including leprosy, which made a person's skin look bad. People who had leprosy were called "lepers."

To find more information on color-coded terms, see pages 261–282.

CONCEPTS | CUSTOMS | GLOSSARY | PEOPLE | PLACES

SEE "Peter's Mother-in-Law Healed of Fever," p. 19.

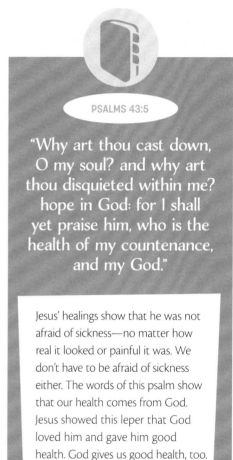

PSALMS 43:5

"Why art thou cast down, O my soul? and why art thou disquieted within me? hope in God: for I shall yet praise him, who is the health of my countenance, and my God."

Jesus' healings show that he was not afraid of sickness—no matter how real it looked or painful it was. We don't have to be afraid of sickness either. The words of this psalm show that our health comes from God. Jesus showed this leper that God loved him and gave him good health. God gives us good health, too.

Lepers had to obey certain Jewish laws. They had to live outside the town. They also had to wear ragged clothes, cover the lower part of their faces, and call out "Unclean! Unclean!" to warn people not to get close to them or touch them. Because of these laws, lepers led sad, lonely lives.

One day a leper came to Jesus. The man kneeled in front of Jesus and said, "If you want to, you can make me clean. You can heal me."

SEE Healing by Touch, p. 267.

Jesus didn't step back from this man the way other people always did. Jesus wasn't afraid of the man or his sickness or the Jewish law that said he shouldn't touch him. Jesus didn't see this man as a leper. He knew that God is Spirit and that man is made in God's image and likeness. So, Jesus saw this man—and everyone—as spiritual and never having anything unlike God.

Then Jesus reached out and gently touched the man as he said, "Of course I want to help you." The man felt loved and cared for—maybe for the first time in a long while.

Jesus knew the man was already the pure, spiritual likeness of God, so he told him, "Be clean." It was like saying, "Be who you really are, be the way God made you." The minute he said this, the man was healed! His skin was smooth and beautiful. He was so happy!

Jesus showed that even leprosy couldn't win out against God's all-powerful good.

Then, speaking firmly to the man, Jesus said, "**Don't tell anyone** about this healing. Go do what the Jewish laws say you should do now that you are healed."

24

The man went on his way to obey the Jewish laws. But he was so happy to be healed that he couldn't be quiet about it. He told everybody he saw that Jesus had healed him.

Then, so many people wanted to see Jesus that he couldn't go into the city for a while. Instead, he had to stay in the country. But, even there, people from all around found him and came to be healed. ■

The **priests** told people who were considered "unclean" or impure what laws or **purification rituals** to follow in order to become "clean" or pure again. See also **Laws of Cleanness**, p. 268.

What can YOU do?

Do you know someone who is sad and lonely? Maybe this person is sick or has a disability, and no one pays attention to him or her. A kind word, a smile, or playing a game together would probably mean a lot to that person. And it would bless you, too. Jesus said, "Love thy neighbour as thyself" (Matthew 22:39). He loved even the people others wouldn't love—and you can, too!

Read a testimony related to this healing on page 241, "Skin Eruption Cleared."

25

MARK 2:1–12

MAN HEALED OF PARALYSIS

You can find other accounts of this healing in Matthew 9:1–8 and Luke 5:17–26.

After healing many people in Galilee, including a leper, 🞉 Jesus traveled from town to town for a while, teaching and healing many others. When he returned to Capernaum, where he had healed a man who was mentally ill, 🞉 the news spread quickly that Jesus was back.

Many people squeezed inside the house where Jesus was staying so they could get near him. 💬 When there was no room for even one more person inside, people stood outside, crowded around the door.

To find more information on color-coded terms, see pages 261–282.

CONCEPTS | CUSTOMS | GLOSSARY | PEOPLE | PLACES

26

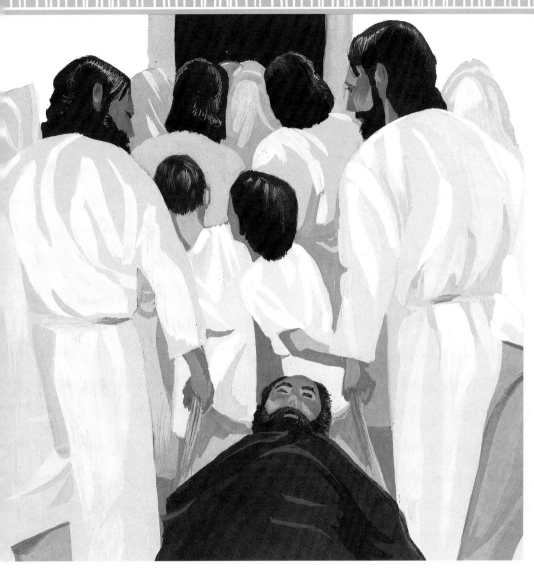

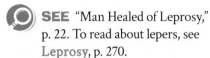 **SEE** "Man Healed of Leprosy," p. 22. To read about lepers, see Leprosy, p. 270.

SEE "Man Healed of Mental Illness (Capernaum)," p. 14.

Luke adds that among the people who came to see Jesus were Pharisees and scribes from Galilee, Judea, and Jerusalem (see Luke 5:17). These men had probably heard about Jesus' healings, the huge crowds that were following him, and the **Sabbath laws** and **laws of cleanness** that he had broken. They may have come because they were curious about his teaching or to see for themselves if he was breaking Jewish laws.

Jesus taught them the **word** of God—that God is all-powerful and loves and cares for everyone.

Just then, four men arrived who really wanted to see Jesus. They were carrying a friend on a bed because he was paralyzed.

They wanted Jesus to heal their friend, but they couldn't get close to the door because of the crowd.

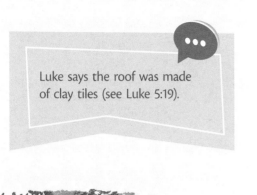

Luke says the roof was made of clay tiles (see Luke 5:19).

Did they give up and go back home?

No! These men must have loved their friend a lot because they never gave up. They were so sure Jesus could heal him that they found a way to get him to Jesus. They carried their friend on his bed up some outside stairs to the roof of the house.

Then they made a hole in the roof. This wasn't too hard to do because most roofs were flat and often made of layers of branches, grasses, and mud placed over wooden beams.

Imagine the people inside the house who were listening to Jesus. They could hear the men on the roof, and soon dirt and sticks started falling down on them. They must have wondered what was going on!

When the hole in the roof was big enough, the men slowly lowered their friend on his bed until he was lying right in front of Jesus! Jesus could see that these men had **faith** in God to heal their friend.

Jesus spoke lovingly to the man, comforting him. He said, "Son, you are forgiven, **healed of your sins.**" 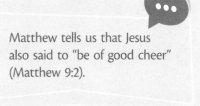 Jesus knew the man needed to hear these words. In those days, people believed that those who were sick or paralyzed were being punished by God because they had sinned, meaning they had done bad things. This man might have been thinking of himself as a sinner.

But Jesus knew this man as God knew him—as God's perfect, spiritual child. He couldn't be bad or paralyzed. Jesus' words helped the man feel God's love. And that love healed him of the thought that he was a bad person. It freed his thought, and it also freed his body.

Hearing that he wasn't a sinner must have made the man so happy! That message probably blessed a lot of people in the crowd, too.

But not everyone liked those words. Some scribes who were there got angry. They heard Jesus' words of comfort and thought to themselves, "How dare Jesus talk that way! He's acting like God by forgiving the man's sins. Only God can forgive sins."

Matthew tells us that Jesus also said to "be of good cheer" (Matthew 9:2).

Luke tells us that both scribes and Pharisees were present (see Luke 5:21).

The scribes and Pharisees thought Jesus' words were **blasphemy**. They thought he was dishonoring God by saying he was as powerful as God.

29

I JOHN 3:9

"Whosoever is born of God doth not commit sin; for his seed remaineth in him: and he cannot sin, because he is born of God."

Jesus knew that we are all created without sin, in the image and likeness of God, who is Spirit. By seeing everyone as completely good and never punished by God, Jesus healed the sick. We can do this too! Seeing ourselves as God sees us heals both sin and sickness.

What can YOU do?

Sometimes when you need help, it might seem impossible to get it. But you can always get help. When you ask God for an answer and then listen, an idea will come—just as it did for these four men. They found a very unusual way to help their friend! You're God's child, and God loves and guides you.

Jesus knew what they were thinking. So he turned to the scribes and said, "Why are you thinking such things? Which is easier to say to this man—'Your sins are forgiven' or 'Get up, pick up your bed, and walk'?"

It would have been easier for Jesus if he hadn't told the man that his sins were forgiven. Jesus wouldn't have gotten into trouble with the scribes if he had simply told the man to stand up, pick up his bed, and walk. But instead of doing what was easy, Jesus said what the man most needed to hear.

Then Jesus told the scribes, "I will show you that the Son of man has power to heal people of sins." Jesus often called himself the "Son of man."

He then turned and looked at the man on the bed. Everyone watched to see what he would do.

Jesus said to the man, "Get up, pick up your bed, and go home." Instantly, the man did it! He stood up, picked up his bed, and walked out through the crowd.

When everyone saw the man walking, they knew the man's sins must have been forgiven, just as Jesus had said.

The crowd was amazed—God's power had healed the man. They praised God, saying, "We've never seen anything like this! Thank you, God!" 💬 ■

Matthew adds that the crowd glorified, or praised, God because God "had given such power unto men" (Matthew 9:8).

MAN WITH WITHERED HAND HEALED

You can find other accounts of this healing in Matthew 12:9–13 and Mark 3:1–5.

Jesus continued healing and teaching in the cities and the countryside. Then, one Sabbath day, when he was in Galilee teaching in a synagogue, several scribes and Pharisees were there, too. But they weren't there to pray and learn about God. They were there to see if they could catch Jesus doing something wrong.

To find more information on color-coded terms, see pages 261–282.

CONCEPTS   CUSTOMS   GLOSSARY   PEOPLE   PLACES

SEE "Man Healed of Mental Illness (Capernaum)," p. 14.

II SAMUEL 22:33

"God is my strength and power: And he maketh my way perfect."

Jesus knew that everyone is perfect and spiritual—created in the image of God. He knew God gives everyone strength and power. Jesus saw this man as God had created him and knew God would never allow him to be less than perfect. This view of the man healed him—instantly. When we see ourselves and others as God has created us, we can see healing take place, too.

They might have been thinking, "When he healed the mentally ill man on the Sabbath, he broke a **Sabbath law**.  Maybe he will heal again on the Sabbath, and if he does, we can find a reason to get rid of him." They didn't want so many people paying attention to Jesus instead of to them.

One of the men in the synagogue had a problem with his right hand—it was withered. Either his hand was not formed in the right way or it was weak and didn't work the way it should.

The scribes and Pharisees began to watch Jesus very closely to see if he would heal the man.

SEE Exodus 20:8.

Matthew adds that Jesus made them think some more when he asked, "If a man had a sheep that fell into a hole on the Sabbath, wouldn't he lift it out?" Everyone knew, of course, that the answer was yes. Jesus then reminded them that a man is worth much more than a sheep (see Matthew 12:11–12). Jesus was pointing out that, no matter what Jewish law said about not working on the Sabbath, people would still help an animal in trouble, so they should help people, too. And a great way to help people is to heal them by seeing them as spiritual and perfect—the way God made them.

Mark adds that Jesus "looked round about on them with anger, being grieved for the hardness of their hearts" (Mark 3:5). Jesus saw how stubborn and unloving the scribes and Pharisees were being. He might have thought, "How sad that they're missing the happiness of helping others on the Sabbath day."

34

Jesus knew what they were thinking. He said to the man with the withered hand, "Stand up and come forward." Probably, Jesus wanted everyone to see what was going to happen.

The man obeyed Jesus and went toward him.

The Pharisees thought Jesus shouldn't heal the man on the Sabbath. But Jesus knew that when he was healing, he was doing God's work. Helping and healing were the best way to obey the Fourth Commandment, "Remember the sabbath day, to keep it holy."

Jesus surprised the scribes and Pharisees by asking them a question: "Does the law command us to do good and help people on the Sabbath or to do evil and hurt people? To save life or to destroy it?"

Jesus looked each scribe and Pharisee in the eye, one by one.

Maybe he was waiting for them to answer his question. But no one said anything.

Jesus then turned back to the man and said to him, "Stretch out your hand!"

Jesus knew that because God is Spirit, God's creation is spiritual. Jesus didn't believe that any part of a child of God could be deformed or weak. All God's children are made perfect, spiritual, and strong.

Then, the man stretched out his hand—and it was just like his other one! A perfect healing on the Sabbath day! ◼

What can YOU do?

The Pharisees tried to stop Jesus from doing good. Sometimes when you're doing something good for someone else—like helping someone who needs a friend—other kids might try to stop you. They might tease you and call you names. If this happens, you can remember that Jesus didn't let anyone stop him from doing good. Nothing can stop you either. When you help others and do what's right, you're doing God's work, and that makes you truly happy.

Read a testimony related to this healing on page 257, "Cold Symptoms Disappear."

NOBLEMAN'S SON HEALED OF ILLNESS

Once, after Jesus had been in Judea for a while, he returned to Galilee, where he visited the town of Cana, up in the hills. 💬

At the same time, 20 miles away in the city of Capernaum, a nobleman, who probably worked for the king, needed help. His son was very sick.

The nobleman had heard that Jesus healed people and that he was in Cana, so he immediately went up the long road to Cana to look for Jesus.

To find more information on color-coded terms, see pages 261–282.

CONCEPTS CUSTOMS GLOSSARY PEOPLE PLACES

When the nobleman found Jesus, he begged him, "Please come down to Capernaum with me and heal my son! He is going to die if you don't come right away."

Jesus said to him, "Unless you people see amazing healings happen, you won't believe."

Jesus might have been talking about the people who came just to watch him heal, not to listen to his teachings. What Jesus really wanted was for people to come to learn more about God and God's loving care for everyone.

The nobleman kept begging Jesus, "Sir, please come down to Capernaum before my child dies!"

Did Jesus leave Cana to go with the man?

No. Jesus wasn't afraid that the boy would die. He knew what was true—that God was this boy's life and that God was keeping him safe. Jesus said to the man, "Go home now. Your son is alive and well."

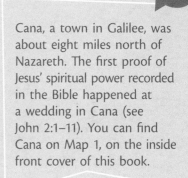

Cana, a town in Galilee, was about eight miles north of Nazareth. The first proof of Jesus' spiritual power recorded in the Bible happened at a wedding in Cana (see John 2:1–11). You can find Cana on Map 1, on the inside front cover of this book.

SEE Faith, p. 263.

JEREMIAH 23:23–24

"Am I a God at hand, saith the Lord, and not a God afar off?... Do not I fill heaven and earth? saith the Lord."

God, who is Spirit and Life, is everywhere. Jesus knew that God's power of good was always right with him. And he knew it is always with each one of God's children, keeping them safe and healthy no matter where they are. That power of good is never far from any of us. It is always right at hand, helping us.

And do you know what? This man, who had been begging Jesus to come with him, believed those words—"Your son is alive and well."

The nobleman wasn't afraid anymore. He knew that God was taking care of his son and that he would live. He didn't have to see his son healed and happy before he believed.

What can YOU do?

Have you ever wanted to help someone far away who was sick or hurt? Well, you certainly can—you can help by praying! Just like the nobleman, you can believe the truth that Jesus knew. He knew that God makes everyone spiritual and that God is always with everyone, keeping us all perfect and healthy. When you believe this and hold on to it, you're praying in a way that helps bring healing to others, wherever they are.

The man headed back home, certain that his son was well.

As the nobleman went down the long, steep road to Capernaum, he saw some of his servants coming toward him.

They probably couldn't wait to tell him the news: "Your son is alive and well!" That's just what Jesus had said!

The nobleman asked them when his son started to get better. "At one o'clock yesterday afternoon, the fever completely left him," they answered.

Then the nobleman knew that his son was healed at the same time Jesus said, "Your son is alive and well." He and his family and all the servants in his house "believed"—they trusted that Jesus healed through the power of God.

What a great day for the nobleman, his son, and everyone in the house!

MATTHEW 8:5–13

CENTURION'S SERVANT HEALED OF PARALYSIS

You can find another account of this healing in Luke 7:1–10.

Jesus had been teaching large crowds and healing lots of people in the countryside of Galilee. Then one day he came back to Capernaum.

The Romans ruled the whole country at that time, and many Roman soldiers lived in Capernaum. 🔍 One of the soldiers, a centurion, came to Jesus for help. "Lord," said the centurion, "my servant is at home in bed paralyzed. He is in great pain." 💬

🔍 **SEE** Roman Empire, p. 281.

💬

Luke adds that the servant, "who was dear unto him, was sick, and ready to die" (Luke 7:2). In Luke's account of the healing, the centurion didn't go to Jesus himself. Instead, he sent some important Jews from the synagogue to ask Jesus to come and heal his servant. The men told Jesus that this centurion was a good man and loved the Jews so much that he had built them a synagogue (see Luke 7:3–5).

To find more information on color-coded terms, see pages 261–282.

CONCEPTS CUSTOMS GLOSSARY PEOPLE PLACES

GENESIS 28:15

"Behold, I am with thee, and will keep thee in all places whither thou goest."

Jesus knew that this is God's promise to each one of us. Even if we seem to be all alone or far from help, God is with us, keeping us safe. No one is ever separated from God's love, care, and healing power.

Healing was one way for Jesus to fulfill the special purpose God had given him, so he replied right away, "I will come and heal him."

The centurion then surprised Jesus.

Instead of leading Jesus to his home, the centurion said, "I'm not good enough for you to come inside my house."

Perhaps the centurion thought he wasn't important enough to have a great teacher and healer like Jesus come to his house. Or maybe the centurion, who was a Gentile, stopped Jesus from coming with him because Jesus was a Jew. The centurion would have known about the Jewish law that said a Jew couldn't go into a Gentile's house, and he wouldn't have wanted Jesus to get in trouble.

But if the centurion didn't think Jesus should come to his house, how did he expect Jesus to heal his servant?

The centurion knew how powerful giving orders can be. He said to Jesus, "Just say the word, and my servant will be healed."

Then he added, "I'm used to taking orders from someone more powerful than I am. And I also know how to give orders. I tell one soldier, 'Go,' and he goes. I tell another soldier, 'Come,' and he comes. I tell my servant, 'Do this,' and he does it."

The centurion knew that just as he had power over his soldiers, Jesus had power over sickness. The centurion got his power from the Roman emperor, while Jesus got his power from God.

Jesus was amazed at what the centurion said. He turned around and told the people following him, "This man's **faith** is very great. I haven't found a faith like this among the Jews." Jesus was saying that the centurion's trust in God's power to heal was much greater than the Jews' trust.

When Jesus finished talking to the people, he turned to the centurion and

Matthew says that Jesus continued to tell the Jews how important it is to have faith. The Jews believed that when the **Messiah** came, he would bring the **kingdom of God**. Jesus wanted the Jews to know that they didn't have to wait for the kingdom of God. If they had faith in God, they could experience the love and goodness of God's kingdom right then.

43

What can YOU do?

Do you have faith that your prayer can heal someone who is sick? Jesus' prayers were powerful because he listened to good thoughts from God. He said "No!" to sickness—he ordered it to stay out of his thinking. You can be like Jesus and fill your thought so full of good ideas from God that there is no room for anything else. God, who is Spirit, makes everyone spiritual, whole, and healthy. It's wonderful to know this truth—and to know that it heals you and others!

Read a testimony related to this healing on page 242, "My Victory over Childhood Paralysis."

said to him, "Go home now. What you had faith in has happened."

And at that very moment, his servant was healed. ■

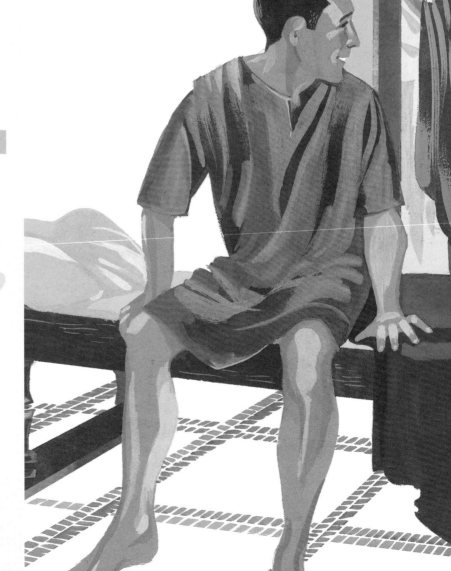

LUKE 7:11–17

WIDOW'S SON BROUGHT BACK TO LIFE

The day after Jesus healed the centurion's servant in Capernaum, he traveled with his disciples about 25 miles up into the hills of Galilee to the city of Nain. Many people followed him.

SEE "Centurion's Servant Healed of Paralysis," p. 41.

To find more information on color-coded terms, see pages 261–282.

CONCEPTS	CUSTOMS	GLOSSARY	PEOPLE	PLACES

45

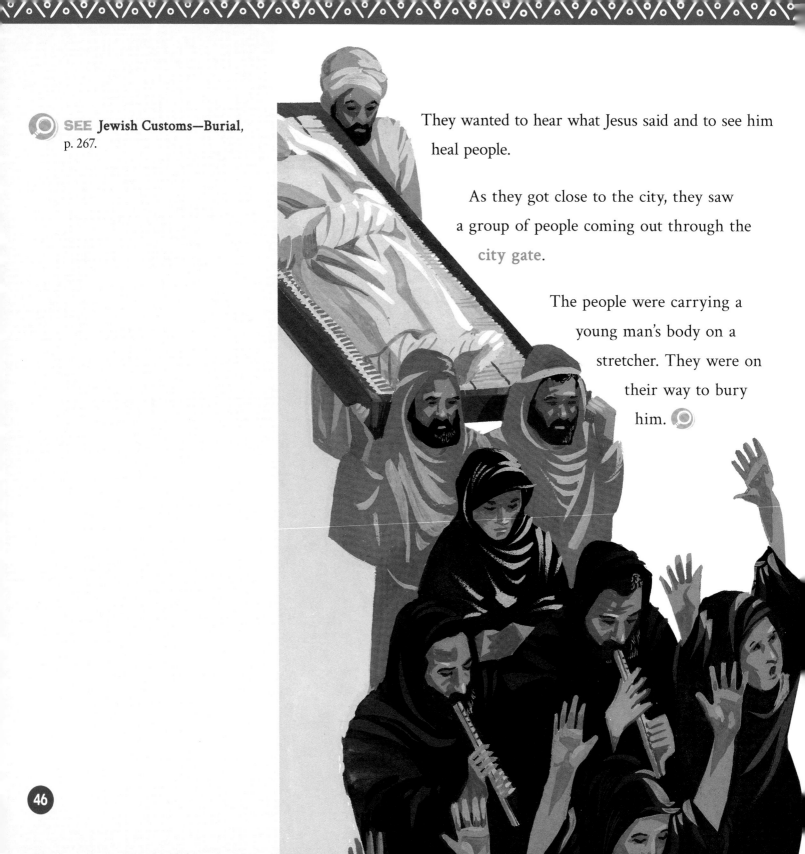

SEE Jewish Customs—Burial, p. 267.

They wanted to hear what Jesus said and to see him heal people.

As they got close to the city, they saw a group of people coming out through the city gate.

The people were carrying a young man's body on a stretcher. They were on their way to bury him.

In those days people showed their sadness about someone's death by crying loudly and playing flutes that made sad sounds.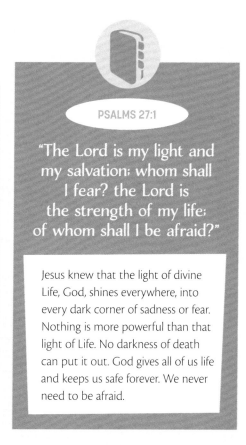

The people were especially sorry for the young man's mother because she was a widow. That means her husband had died. This young man was the woman's only son.

When Jesus saw the mother crying, he felt tender care for her. He said to her lovingly but firmly, "Don't cry." He knew she didn't have to be sad. God doesn't take away life—God gives life.

○ **SEE Jewish Customs—Mourning**, p. 268.

○ **SEE** Woman/Women, p. 278.

PSALMS 27:1

"The Lord is my light and my salvation; whom shall I fear? the Lord is the strength of my life; of whom shall I be afraid?"

Jesus knew that the light of divine Life, God, shines everywhere, into every dark corner of sadness or fear. Nothing is more powerful than that light of Life. No darkness of death can put it out. God gives all of us life and keeps us safe forever. We never need to be afraid.

 **SEE** Laws of Cleanness—Death, p. 268.

What can YOU do?

When you're crying because you're sad or hurt, it helps to stop crying and be quiet. Then you're more able to hear God's messages and feel God's love and comfort. If it feels hard to calm down, you can ask God to help you. God is always giving you peace and helping you feel Love's presence right there with you. Being calm is natural when you know God is with you.

Then Jesus put his hand on the stretcher. The men carrying it were shocked—and stood still.

Everyone knew there were rules against touching the bed of a dead person. But Jesus didn't let those rules keep him from healing the man. He knew that God is divine Life. And he knew that death has no power over God's children because they are made to be like God, spiritual and alive forever.

Jesus very calmly gave this strong command: "Young man, I tell you, get up!"

And the young man sat up. He began talking right away, and Jesus brought him to his mother.

The people were filled with wonder! They praised God, saying, "A great prophet has come to be with us again.  God is taking care of us."

After that, everywhere the people went, they talked about the amazing healing they had seen that day. ■

When Jesus brought this young man to life, the people may have realized that Jesus was the great prophet Moses had said would come (see Deuteronomy 18:15).

WOMAN HEALED OF SIN

Jesus was in Galilee, where he had brought a young man back to life.  While he was there, a Pharisee named Simon invited him to dinner at his home.

Pharisees like Simon did their best to obey the Ten Commandments from God, but they also followed hundreds of other Jewish laws. The Pharisees thought these other laws helped them obey the Commandments.

SEE "Widow's Son Brought Back to Life," p. 45.

To find more information on color-coded terms, see pages 261–282.

| CONCEPTS | CUSTOMS | GLOSSARY | PEOPLE | PLACES |

But over the years, they began to pay more attention to these other Jewish laws than to the Commandments. They also watched everyone else to make sure they were obeying all the Jewish laws.

Like the Pharisees, Jesus obeyed the Commandments. But, unlike the Pharisees, he knew that what was most important about the Commandments was love—love for God and for others. So when Jesus had to choose between obeying a Jewish law or being loving and healing others, Jesus chose to love.

People had been calling Jesus a prophet, someone who hears God's directions and shares them with others. Simon probably agreed that this is what a prophet should do. But Simon also thought a prophet should obey all the Jewish laws.

Simon may have invited Jesus to his house to find out if Jesus obeyed these laws. If he didn't obey them, Simon would probably think that Jesus wasn't a prophet.

Dinner parties were held either inside the house or outside in an open courtyard. Food was served on mats on the floor or on low tables. Guests sat or lay on mats, cushions, or couches. Most people were welcome to come to dinner parties, even if they weren't invited. They couldn't sit with the guests or eat the food, but they could sit against the walls, watch the guests eat, and listen to them talk.

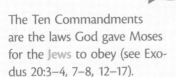

The Ten Commandments are the laws God gave Moses for the Jews to obey (see Exodus 20:3–4, 7–8, 12–17).

The woman is not named in this story. Traditionally, she has been called "Mary Magdalene," but she is not at all like Mary Magdalene in the Bible. The woman in this story was healed of sin. There is no reason to think that Mary Magdalene was ever a sinner. The Bible says Jesus healed Mary Magdalene of seven **demons** (see Mark 16:9; Luke 8:1–3). This probably refers to how serious her problem was rather than to sin.

During Simon's dinner party, a woman came in who was not welcome. People knew about this woman and thought of her as a sinner who had done many bad things.

When she came in, the woman didn't sit against the wall and watch. She went right up to Jesus and stood by his feet. Big tears began to roll down her cheeks.

As this woman cried softly, she kneeled and washed Jesus' feet with her tears. The woman had no towel, so she used her long hair to tenderly dry Jesus' feet. Then she kissed them. Next, she opened a small bottle of perfumed oil she had with her. She gently poured this special oil on Jesus' feet.

As Simon watched this woman taking care of Jesus, he thought to himself, "If Jesus were really a prophet, he would know this woman is a sinner. A prophet would know better than to let someone who has done bad things come close to him—and certainly he wouldn't let this woman touch him."

Jesus knew what Simon was thinking.

He said, "Simon, I have something to tell you."

"Of course, Teacher," replied Simon. "Tell me."

Jesus then told Simon a story to help him become more loving. Jesus told him about two men who borrowed money from a banker. One borrowed 500 silver coins, and the other borrowed 50 silver coins. But neither one could pay him back. The banker surprised them both by telling them he forgave them. That meant they never had to pay him back.

Then Jesus asked Simon which of these men would love the banker more. Simon answered that it would be the one who owed the most, because he had been forgiven the most. Jesus said he was right.

To help Simon learn from the story, Jesus pointed out that the woman at the dinner party had treated him more lovingly than Simon had.

Jesus told Simon, "When I came into your house, you didn't give me water for my feet. But this woman washed my feet with her tears and dried them with her hair. You didn't kiss me, but this

The Bible calls this an "alabaster box of ointment" (Luke 7:37). In Greek this can mean either a jar of ointment or a bottle of perfumed oil.

SEE **Laws of Cleanness—Sin**, p. 268.

Here's one way to look at Jesus' story: The debtor who owed 500 coins was like the woman. The other debtor was like Simon. The coins stand for how much they wanted to be forgiven or healed of their sins. The woman's great love showed that she had turned away from her mistakes and been healed of her sins. Simon's small amount of love showed that he didn't even know he needed to be healed of sin. When Jesus pointed out that the woman had shown love and respect for Jesus in more ways than Simon had, Jesus was trying to help Simon see that he was like the man in the story who loved little.

MATTHEW 22:37–39

"Thou shalt love the Lord thy God with all thy heart, and with all thy soul, and with all thy mind. This is the first and great commandment. And the second is like unto it, Thou shalt love thy neighbour as thyself."

Jesus told his followers that all they needed to do to obey the commandments was to love God and love others. When we are loving God, we're not letting anything into our thinking except God's love and its power. And when we are loving others, we're seeing them as God sees them—as the pure and perfect children of Love. Jesus loved people no matter who they were, where they came from, or what they had done. When Jesus loved this woman by seeing only the goodness of God in her, she was healed. We can heal as Jesus healed when we love as Jesus loved.

SEE Jewish Customs—Guests, p. 267.

SEE Blasphemy, p. 270.

woman hasn't stopped kissing my feet. You didn't put olive oil on my head, but this woman poured perfumed oil on my feet."

Then Jesus said to Simon, "This woman's sins are forgiven, for her love is very great."

Simon probably wondered why Jesus was praising this woman for being loving since, to Simon, she was a sinner. But Jesus saw her as she truly was, as a perfect child of God. And he wanted to help Simon see her that way too.

Jesus knew the truth that God's children are always good and pure, just as God has made them. This truth helped people feel their own goodness. Then, they were able to do what was right. Any bad thoughts, or sins, were wiped out—healed by the power of God's love and truth. That's what happened to this woman.

Jesus could tell she had a deep love for the goodness and purity that he taught and lived. Her tears showed her sorrow for the bad things she had thought and done. Her kisses showed her meekness and her willingness to understand Jesus' teachings. The oil she poured on Jesus' feet showed that she was grateful to be near this loving man. Jesus knew that her thought had changed and that she was **healed of her sins**.

Like this woman, Simon had also sinned, but, unlike her, he didn't know it. He had sinned by not being kind to Jesus, who was a guest in his home, and by thinking he was better than the woman. Jesus was trying to show Simon that his lack of love meant he needed to change his thinking and be healed of his sin.

Then, right there in front of the people at the dinner, Jesus said to the woman, "You are healed of your sins." Simon's guests didn't understand this. They said to themselves, "Who does this man think he is, healing people of sins?"

Next, Jesus said to the woman, "Your **faith** has saved you." The way she had treated him showed how sorry she was for the things she had done, and Jesus saw her goodness and purity.

She left the house that day with this loving message from Jesus, "Go in **peace**." ■

What can YOU do?

If you meet people who look or act so different that others don't want to be with them, what can you do? You might think about what Jesus would do. Jesus loved people and looked for God's goodness in them. You can do that, too. Loving others and seeing God's goodness in them brings healing and peace to them—and to you, too.

MATTHEW 12:22–23

MAN HEALED OF BLINDNESS AND MUTENESS

You can find another account of this healing in Luke 11:14.

Jesus was in Galilee, where he was teaching and healing people.

To find more information on color-coded terms, see pages 261–282.

CONCEPTS CUSTOMS GLOSSARY PEOPLE PLACES

A man was brought to him who couldn't see or talk. 💬
Almost everyone believed that a **demon**, or evil spirit, had made him that way.

Matthew and Luke both say the man was dumb, or mute, which means he couldn't talk (see Matthew 12:22; Luke 11:14). Matthew says the man was also blind.

JOHN 8:32

"Ye shall know the truth, and the truth shall make you free."

Jesus told his disciples that if they learned the truth he taught and lived their lives using this truth, it would make them free. We can also prove that the truth heals, just as Jesus and his disciples did. We can know the truth—that God, good, is the only presence and power and that we are all made in God's image and likeness. Since God, Spirit, is perfect, we're spiritual and perfect. No matter what we see with our eyes, the only true things are what God gives us—perfection, goodness, joy, love, health. Knowing the truth with all our heart and trusting God's goodness and love brings healing. Just as the truth set people free from sickness, sin, and death in Jesus' time, the truth sets us and others free today.

57

What can YOU do?

You may know someone with a problem that seems too hard to heal in an instant. If so, you can know that God, who is entirely good, is infinite. That means God, good, is everywhere. Just think of it! With God's goodness everywhere, there's no room left for anything bad.

When Jesus saw something that looked bad or wrong, he shut out thoughts about the problem and filled his thinking with the truth that God, good, is everywhere. He trusted this truth and didn't doubt it. As a result, people were healed, just as this man was. He could see and talk right away.

You can know what Jesus knew. And you can heal instantly, too. God's goodness fills all space and every moment, always and forever. Each moment God is giving you good thoughts that help you know what is true and real. Those good thoughts are just as powerful to heal today as they were in Jesus' time.

But Jesus didn't believe this. He knew that all God's children are made happy and healthy. Demons, or evil spirits, are only bad thoughts or lies. It's a lie that a child of God can't see or talk. Jesus knew that God is Love and tenderly cares for everyone. God's children are made in Love's likeness—spiritual, free, and perfect. This was the truth about this man.

When the man was brought to Jesus, the truth Jesus knew healed him instantly. The man could see clearly and talk perfectly. Can you imagine how happy he was?

The people were so amazed at this wonderful healing that they asked each other whether Jesus was the Son of David, the Messiah. ■

LUKE 8:22–39

MAN HEALED OF MENTAL ILLNESS
— (Gadara) —

You can find other accounts of this healing in Matthew 8:23–34 and Mark 4:35–5:20.

Jesus had been teaching and healing people in Galilee, in the towns and countryside near the beautiful lake called the Sea of Galilee. Then one day he got into a boat with his disciples and said, "Let's go to the other side of the lake." So they started off.

During the trip, a big storm came up. The wind was very strong, and the waves were so high that the disciples were afraid the boat

To find more information on color-coded terms, see pages 261–282.

CONCEPTS CUSTOMS GLOSSARY PEOPLE PLACES

would turn over. But Jesus wasn't afraid. He ordered the wind and waves to be still. And they were!

Then Jesus and his disciples continued their trip across the lake.

Soon, they arrived in the land of the Gadarenes in **Decapolis**, where many **Gentiles** lived. 💬 Since most Gentiles didn't believe in the one God or follow God's laws, **Jews** avoided them. But Jesus loved everyone.

When they got to the shore, a man came toward Jesus shouting. 💬 This man had been mentally ill for a long time. He wasn't wearing any clothes, and he was wild and very loud, just as the thundering storm on the lake had been.

The man didn't live in a house. Instead, he stayed in dark **caves**. Sometimes he was so out of control that people tied his hands and feet with chains to try to calm him down. But he was so strong

that he would break the chains and run into the wilderness. 💬

In those days people were superstitious. 💿 They thought there were powers other than God that could hurt them or help them, but they never knew when these powers would act or what they would do. People also believed in **demons**, or unclean spirits. They thought these demons, or spirits, were invisible beings that could make them sick or mentally ill.

People thought demons were making this man wild and out of control. But Jesus didn't believe that. He knew that what people called demons were just bad or wild thoughts that had no power.

What would Jesus do when he met this man?

The exact location of this healing is not known. Matthew says the people were called "Gergesenes," meaning that they came from the town of Gergesa on the Sea of Galilee (see Matthew 8:28). Mark and Luke say that the people were called "Gadarenes," meaning that they came from Gadara or an area around Gadara, which is in the region of Decapolis (see Mark 5:1; Luke 8:26).

Matthew says there were two wild men who were "exceeding fierce, so that no man might pass by that way" (Matthew 8:28).

Mark adds that the man was so unhappy that he screamed and cut himself with sharp stones (see Mark 5:5).

💿 SEE **Laws of Cleanness**, p. 268.

Matthew, Mark, and Luke often describe Jesus as "casting out devils," or **demons**. Jesus never believed demons were real. He knew they were only bad thoughts. And he helped people see that God's power of good is the only power. The Bible tells us that Jesus cast out demons, or bad thoughts, by God's "**word**" and by the "Spirit of God" (see Matthew 8:16; Matthew 12:28).

Jesus knew that God gave him the ability and authority to get rid of any thought that was not good. His understanding that God is the only power helped remove people's fears. And when their fears were gone, so were their diseases and sins. The Bible calls this "casting out devils," or demons. Today we might call it "casting out evil"—getting rid of bad thoughts by understanding that only good is real and present.

The first thing Jesus did was to give a strong order: "Come out of the man, you unclean spirit!"

As Jesus looked at this man, he saw what others didn't see. He saw the man God had created—calm, able to think clearly, and in control of himself. Jesus knew there is only one Spirit, which is God—and this calm, peaceful Spirit is everywhere. There is no room for any other spirit. God doesn't create unclean spirits, or wild thoughts and actions. All that God creates is good, and God creates all that is real.

When Jesus told the unclean spirit to leave, the man fell down at Jesus' feet. He shouted, "What do you want with me,

Jesus, Son of the Most High God? I beg you—don't bother me."

"Son of the Most High God" was another name for "Messiah" or "**Christ**."

This man could probably tell that Jesus had the power to cast out demons. But at that moment, maybe the man didn't think demons, or wild thoughts, were controlling him. He probably believed it was normal for him to be wild, so he wanted to be left alone.

But Jesus cared about the man. He wouldn't leave him, and he wouldn't give up on him. Jesus wasn't fooled by the wild thoughts

because he knew they were just lies. He knew that only God was in control of this man's thinking, and he wanted to help the man see this, too.

Jesus must have been praying, listening for what God was telling him to do, because he faced this man calmly and asked him, "What is your name?" People's names had special meaning in those days. Their names told what they were like or what their nature was. Jesus was asking the man to think about what he believed about himself.

The man said his name was "Legion." But that's not a name. The word "legion" means a group of about six thousand soldiers.

Maybe Jesus' question helped the man see that he had let many demons, or wild thoughts, get him so mixed up that he had forgotten who he really was. The question may have made him think about his real name and true nature. At that point, he probably realized those demons were not part of him, and he wanted them out of his life.

And right there in front of him was Jesus—the perfect person to help him.

People were very afraid of "the deep," or "the abyss." Some believed the deep was the place of the dead, or hell.

Instead of mentioning "the deep," Mark says that the man didn't want the demons to go "out of the country," which means areas where no one lived (Mark 5:10).

Jesus knew the man wanted to be healed. But the man still thought demons were real, and he was afraid of them. He might have believed he had to keep them happy so they wouldn't hurt him.

The man thought one way to get rid of the demons was for them to go to a place called "the deep." But this probably didn't seem like a good choice to the man. Like many other people at that time, he believed the deep was a place where the demons would be punished. So he thought they wouldn't want to go there and might hurt him if they were sent there. He even said out loud not to send the demons into the deep.

The man thought it would be better to get rid of the demons by having them go into the herd of pigs on the hill nearby. He believed the demons would be happy to go into the pigs and wouldn't hurt him when they did.

Jesus knew the man wasn't completely ready to let go of his beliefs about demons. Jesus didn't try to make him understand everything at once. He knew that sometimes people have to take one step at a time in order to give up old beliefs and understand God and God's great power. So Jesus let the man believe the demons had gone into the pigs.

When the pigs suddenly ran down the steep hillside into the lake, the man believed the demons were destroyed. He was very

The Bible describes what the man said as the demons talking to Jesus (see Luke 8:31–32). But this is impossible because demons, or unclean spirits, are not real, so they can't speak. When the Bible says that the demons talked to Jesus, it means that the mentally ill man spoke aloud what he believed the demons were saying, because he thought they controlled his thinking and spoke through him.

Mark says the herd consisted of two thousand swine, or pigs (see Mark 5:13). Before pigs were tamed and cared for by herders, they ran wild and were called boars. We don't know what the pigs in this story looked like, but a wild boar could weigh as much as 400 pounds. It had long bristles, five-inch tusks that were very sharp, and a long nose used for digging up roots to eat. Boars could be frightened easily and could run very fast.

Since mostly **Gentiles** lived in this country, the pig herders were probably Gentiles who, unlike the **Jews**, did not believe they would become "unclean" by herding pigs.

JAMES 4:7

"Resist the devil, and he will flee from you."

Jesus knew that what people called demons, or devils, were only bad or wild thoughts and that God gives everyone the strength to resist, or stand up to, bad thoughts. When Jesus told the demon, or unclean spirit, to come out of the man, he was showing his understanding of God's power. This understanding is like a bright light chasing away the darkness. God gives us all the strength we need to say "No!" to bad thoughts. Then, they disappear for us, too.

superstitious. He needed to see the pigs run into the lake in order to believe he was free of the demons.

But Jesus had always known that demons were not real. He knew they didn't have any power over this man and couldn't move from one place to another. Jesus knew that God, Spirit, is the only power and is everywhere. Demons, or wild thoughts, have no power and no place to be.

From the first time Jesus met this man, he saw only a perfect man, made in the pure, spiritual likeness of God, who is Spirit. By seeing this man as God's likeness, Jesus healed him.

As soon as the man believed the demons were gone, he was free of fear. He was ready for the next step. He was ready to learn about God's all-power and about himself as the child of God.

The pig herders, who saw what had happened, ran to tell other people. Many from the countryside and the town hurried to see for themselves.

They could hardly believe what they saw! The wild man they had all been so afraid of wasn't wild anymore. He was sitting quietly and peacefully at Jesus' feet, listening to him teach, the same way a disciple would. The man was dressed and was in his right mind—thinking calm, good thoughts.

The man was completely healed.

When the superstitious people saw that this man was healed, they were afraid because they didn't understand how this healing had happened. They asked Jesus to go back across the lake to his home. So Jesus and the disciples began to get into their boat.

The man who had been healed was so thankful that he begged to go with Jesus. But Jesus had something else important for him to do.

What can YOU do?

Some kids you know might believe in different kinds of superstitions. They might talk to you about evil spirits, demons, ghosts, or haunted houses. Or they might talk to you about luck—either good luck or bad luck. Some might think it's good luck to pick a certain number or wear a special charm. Others might believe it's bad luck to see a black cat or to walk under a ladder.

These kids may just be joking or trying to scare you, or they may really believe that these superstitions are true. Jesus knew that evil spirits and superstitions are not real and have no power. God is the only Spirit, and Spirit has all power and is all good. And because God's power of good governs you every minute, superstition of any kind is no part of your life. When you know this, nothing can scare you, because you are right in the center of God's love. And you can help other kids know this, too!

Read
a testimony related to this healing on page 256, "Symptoms of Learning Disabilities Healed."

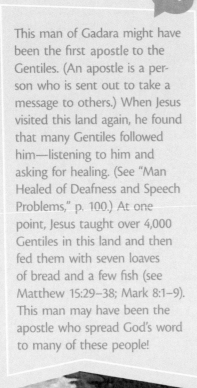

Mark adds that the man began to tell people throughout Decapolis about his wonderful healing and about Jesus. According to Mark, when the people heard the man tell his story, they marveled, which means they were amazed (see Mark 5:20).

This man of Gadara might have been the first apostle to the Gentiles. (An apostle is a person who is sent out to take a message to others.) When Jesus visited this land again, he found that many Gentiles followed him—listening to him and asking for healing. (See "Man Healed of Deafness and Speech Problems," p. 100.) At one point, Jesus taught over 4,000 Gentiles in this land and then fed them with seven loaves of bread and a few fish (see Matthew 15:29–38; Mark 8:1–9). This man may have been the apostle who spread God's word to many of these people!

"Go back to your home," Jesus told the man. "Tell the people there what great things God has done for you."

And that's exactly what the man did! Not only did he tell his friends and family, but he went throughout his city telling everyone that Jesus had healed him. He must have loved going around sharing his good news!

JAIRUS' DAUGHTER BROUGHT BACK TO LIFE

You can find other accounts of this healing in Matthew 9:18–19, 23–26 and Luke 8:40–42, 49–56.

After Jesus healed a man in Gadara of mental illness, he and his disciples crossed the Sea of Galilee and returned to Capernaum.

When they got to the shore, a big crowd was waiting for Jesus.

SEE "Man Healed of Mental Illness (Gadara)," p. 59.

*To find more information on
color-coded terms, see pages 261–282.*

CONCEPTS | CUSTOMS | GLOSSARY | PEOPLE | PLACES

They were all so happy he was back in town. One of the people in the crowd was a man named Jairus. He was the ruler of the synagogue, the place where the Jews met to learn about God. Jairus' job as a ruler, or leader, was to take care of the synagogue and to be in charge of the meetings held there.

Jairus needed help. He fell down at Jesus' feet and begged him, saying, "My little daughter is dying.  Please come and heal her. I want her to live!"

Jairus must have known that Jesus was a great healer because right in or near Capernaum, Jesus had healed people of mental illness, fever, paralysis, a withered hand, and probably many other problems.

Jesus was ready and willing to heal, so he agreed to go with Jairus,

Matthew says that Jairus told Jesus his daughter was already dead (see Matthew 9:18).

Matthew and Mark tell us that Jairus asked Jesus to come and lay his hands on his daughter so that she would be healed (see Matthew 9:18; Mark 5:23). See **Healing by Touch**, p. 267.

SEE the following stories:
- "Man Healed of Mental Illness (Capernaum)," p. 14
- "Peter's Mother-in-Law Healed of Fever," p. 19
- "Man Healed of Paralysis," p. 26
- "Man with Withered Hand Healed," p. 32

which made Jairus very happy! Now, he had hope that his daughter, who was twelve years old, would be healed.

As Jesus started walking with Jairus to his house, lots of people followed him and crowded around him. One of the people on the edge of the crowd was a woman who had been sick for many years.  Moving through the crowd and coming up

SEE "Woman Healed of Illness," p. 76.

These three disciples were the closest to Jesus. He could trust them to pray quietly even when they didn't understand everything Jesus said or did. Jesus chose them to be with him on several special occasions. See, for example, Matthew 17:1–9; Mark 14:32–34.

behind Jesus, she reached out and touched his cloak. As soon as she did this, she knew she was healed.

Jesus stopped and turned to the woman to tell her that her **faith** had healed her. While he was talking, a messenger from Jairus' house came with some very bad news. He told Jairus, "Your daughter is dead. Why bother the teacher anymore?"

The minute Jesus heard this, he said to Jairus, "Don't be afraid. Just keep believing." Jesus wanted Jairus to keep his faith that his daughter would be healed.

Jairus had just seen the woman healed and heard Jesus say that her faith had healed her. This must have given Jairus hope and helped him see that he could have faith that his daughter would be brought back to life.

Jesus went with Jairus to his house but let only three of his disciples—Peter, James, and John —come with them.

When they got to the house, people were there crying very loudly. Others were playing flutes that made sad sounds. This was their way of letting others in the neighborhood know that the girl had died and of showing how sad they were.

Jesus went into the house and said something to the people that surprised them. He asked, "Why are you crying and making such a fuss? She's not dead. She's just asleep."

The people knew the girl was dead, so they couldn't understand why Jesus said she was sleeping. They laughed and made fun of him for saying something that made no sense to them.

But Jesus knew that death was not the end of life. This death that seemed so real was like sleep that the girl could wake up from. Jesus shut out the idea of death and listened to God's thoughts—thoughts

SEE Jewish Customs—Mourning, p. 268.

SEE Laws of Cleanness—Death, p. 268.

73

Jesus' native language was Aramaic. The Bible uses the Aramaic words *Talitha cumi* here (Mark 5:41). *Talitha* means "little girl" and *cumi* means "rise up" or "stand."

Luke adds that "her spirit came again" (Luke 8:55). The word "spirit" in Greek is *pneuma* and can also mean "breath" or "life."

It must have been hard to keep quiet about such a wonderful healing. Matthew says that the news about the girl's experience spread throughout the area (see Matthew 9:26).

of life and love and joy. He knew that God was in control. He also knew that God is Life and that God gives to everyone life, not death.

Next, Jesus did something else that must have surprised the people.

He made the crowd leave the house. Perhaps he did this because he didn't want anyone around who didn't believe in the power of God to bring this girl back to life. He wanted the house to be filled with good thoughts.

Jesus then led the girl's father and mother and his three disciples into the room where the girl was lying. Jesus walked to the girl and took her by the hand as if he were waking her. Then he said to her, "Little girl, get up!"

And, instantly, the girl got up and walked!

Everyone in the room was amazed. They might have wanted to rush out and tell everyone all about it.

But Jesus said, "**Don't tell anyone.**" He probably wanted them to be thankful in a quiet way for God's love and great goodness.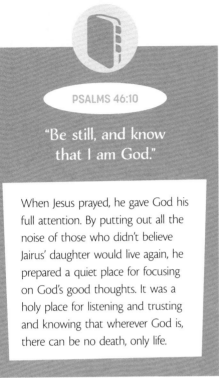

Next, he told them to get her something to eat. Everyone there could see that the girl was just fine.

Imagine how happy her mother and father were that their daughter was alive and completely well! ■

What can YOU do?

When you're not feeling well, think of what Jesus did when he was with Jairus' daughter. He made sure the girl's home was quiet and peaceful. You can be quiet and peaceful, too. You can say to any thoughts that are sad or scary, "Get out!" Then you're ready to hear God's good thoughts and to stand up for what is true about yourself as God's child. And you'll find yourself well!

WOMAN HEALED OF ILLNESS

You can find other accounts of this healing in Matthew 9:20–22 and Luke 8:43–48.

Jesus and his disciples were in Capernaum when, on their way to Jairus' house, a woman needed Jesus' help.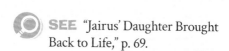

She had been sick for twelve years. Even though she had spent all her money on doctors—hoping they would cure her—none of them could help. In fact, she felt even worse. She probably wondered if she would ever be well again.

SEE "Jairus' Daughter Brought Back to Life," p. 69.

The Bible says this woman had "an issue of blood" (Matthew 9:20; Mark 5:25; Luke 8:43). In Greek, the original language of the New Testament, the phrase means "flow of blood."

To find more information on color-coded terms, see pages 261–282.

| CONCEPTS | CUSTOMS | GLOSSARY | PEOPLE | PLACES |

Besides being sick, the woman was treated very unkindly by other people. They didn't want her to touch them or even get near them because a Jewish law said that anyone who had a sickness like this was "unclean."  She must have felt very lonely.

This woman had heard about Jesus and how he healed people through God's power. She went toward the crowd that was following him, thinking to herself, "If only I can touch his clothes, I'll be well."

Even though she knew people didn't want to be near her, she bravely slipped into the crowd. Without a word, she moved up behind Jesus, reached out, and touched the tassels, or fringe, on his cloak. The minute she did this, she was healed—and she knew it right away.

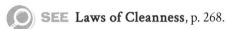 SEE Laws of Cleanness, p. 268.

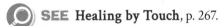 SEE Healing by Touch, p. 267.

Matthew says the woman "touched the hem of his garment" (Matthew 9:20). Luke says she "touched the border of his garment" (Luke 8:44). In Greek, the "hem" or "border" means "tassels" or "fringe." Jesus was probably wearing a large piece of wool material called a cloak. Some cloaks had tassels tied with blue thread at each of the four corners. The Jews believed the tassels were very holy and were meant to remind them of God's law and their duty to obey this law (see Numbers 15:37–41).

Mark says that "the fountain of her blood was dried up" (Mark 5:29). Luke says that "her issue of blood stanched" (Luke 8:44). Both phrases mean that the bleeding stopped.

Both Mark and Luke say that Jesus knew "virtue" had gone out of him (Mark 5:30; Luke 8:46). This word can also mean "power."

GENESIS 1:26, 31

"And God said, Let us make man in our image, after our likeness. . . . And God saw every thing that he had made, and, behold, it was very good."

Jesus knew that God is Spirit. Therefore, everyone is the image and likeness (or reflection) of Spirit. Everyone is spiritual and is always good and perfect. Jesus kept his thought close to God. Even in a crowd of strangers, Jesus knew that each person was God's reflection, good and perfect. Good thoughts like this are powerful. They heal. What Jesus knew then is the truth about everyone—now and forever. We can know this truth and heal too.

Jesus knew it right away, too. He knew his understanding of God had healed someone. Jesus understood that we are all created in the likeness of God. This means God's children are perfect, healthy, and whole—and God keeps them that way.

As soon as Jesus realized someone had been healed, he turned around and asked, "Who touched my clothes?"

His disciples said to him, "How can you ask who touched you? Lots of people are touching and pushing you."

Jesus didn't answer the disciples. Instead, he kept looking around to see who had touched him and been healed.

The woman must have been amazed at her quick healing—and very thankful for it. But she was also afraid to say that she was the one who had touched Jesus. Women didn't usually speak in public. She was also afraid because she had broken the Jewish law that said an unclean person should not touch other people because it would make them unclean, too. She didn't know what Jesus and the others would do if they found out what she had done.

But she had just been healed by Jesus and must have realized that this loving man would be kind to her. That feeling was stronger than her fears, so she came forward and fell down at Jesus' feet. She told him why she had touched his cloak and that she had been healed right away.

Jesus spoke lovingly to her, calling her the sweet name of "daughter."  His great kindness healed her fears.

Then Jesus said to the woman, "Your faith has made you well." He wanted her to know that the tassels she had touched had no healing power. God had healed her.

Matthew and Luke add that Jesus told the woman, "Be of good comfort" (Matthew 9:22; Luke 8:48). The word "comfort" in Greek means "to have courage" or "to be of good cheer."

What can YOU do?

If others are unkind to you, you might feel sad and lonely just as this woman did. You can know that God is your Father-Mother and your best friend. God is always loving you. Ask God, with all your heart, to help you feel divine Love. Listen for the good thoughts God gives you. Look for good wherever you are. Each time you hear or see something good, even if it seems very small, it shows that God's goodness and love are right where you are. You'll soon find that God's love is always bigger than any sadness or loneliness or unkindness—and you'll find friendship and happiness.

The woman's faith was strong. She never gave up hope. She trusted that if Jesus used God's power to heal others, he could heal her, too. She expected to be healed, and she was!

Then Jesus said a wonderful "goodbye" to the woman that would help her know God would always take care of her. He said, "Go in peace. Be free and be well!" ■

MATTHEW 9:27–31

TWO MEN HEALED OF BLINDNESS

Jesus was in Capernaum where he brought a young girl back to life. When he left the girl's house, two blind men followed him, begging him for help. They called out, "Have mercy on us, Son of David!" They were hoping Jesus would be kind and heal them. The name they called Jesus—"Son of David"—means "Messiah," or "Christ." Like many Jews, these men believed the Messiah was a special king that God would send to help and heal them.

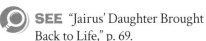 **SEE** "Jairus' Daughter Brought Back to Life," p. 69.

To find more information on color-coded terms, see pages 261–282.

| CONCEPTS | CUSTOMS | GLOSSARY | PEOPLE | PLACES |

What can YOU do?

God is good and the only power, so you can expect good to happen just as these men did. That's what faith is—believing in God's goodness and expecting to experience it. Faith helps us hear God's messages loud and clear. Faith brings healing. You can help others have faith in the power of good, too!

Jesus went into a house, and the blind men followed him. Jesus talked quietly to the men, asking them, "Do you believe that I can heal you?" He wanted to help them see that it was important to have **faith**—to expect healing. They were very sure about their answer. They said, "Yes, Lord!"

Jesus then touched their eyes. This was a loving way to let them know he cared about them. Jesus didn't believe that blindness was the truth about these men. He knew that God, who is Spirit, sees everyone as spiritual and perfect.

As he touched them, Jesus said, "You believed you could be healed, and you are healed!" And they were! Think of how very happy they were to be able to see!

What Jesus said next may have surprised them.

He gave them a strong order. He said, "**Don't tell anyone** about this."

But the men were so happy to be able to see that it was hard for them to obey Jesus. They wanted to tell everyone about their healing. And they did. Everywhere they went, they told how Jesus had healed them and how wonderful it was to be able to see. ■

SEE **Healing by Touch**, p. 267.

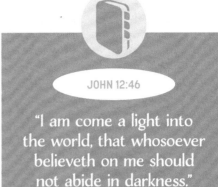

JOHN 12:46

"I am come a light into the world, that whosoever believeth on me should not abide in darkness."

Jesus had complete faith in the truth that everyone is made in God's image and, therefore, is always spiritual, good, and perfect. This truth of our spiritual nature is like light. When a light is turned on, darkness disappears, and we can see that darkness is nothing. When the truth of our spiritual nature fills our thought, the darkness of sickness, sin, and death disappears, and we are healed. Jesus proved this when he healed the two blind men instantly. Today, we have this same light of truth to help us. No matter how dark the trouble may seem, we can shine the light of truth on it and see that trouble disappear.

Read a testimony related to this healing on page 246, "Seeing Clearly."

83

MAN HEALED OF MUTENESS

Jesus had spent the day healing people in Capernaum. Early in the day he healed a woman who had been ill for many years. Then he brought a 12-year-old girl back to life. As he left her home, two blind men followed him into another house, and he healed them, too.

As the two men left, feeling very happy to be able to see, Jesus must have thanked God for this power to bless so many people.

To find more information on
color-coded terms, see pages 261–282.

CONCEPTS CUSTOMS GLOSSARY PEOPLE PLACES

He knew his purpose was to heal and to teach others to heal. He once said, "The Father has not left me alone, for I always do what pleases him."

Just then, people brought someone else who needed healing to Jesus. This man was mute, which means he couldn't talk.

In those days people believed in invisible beings called **demons**. And they believed that a demon was keeping this man from being able to speak.

But Jesus knew that demons aren't real. He knew they are just bad thoughts that have no power because God and God's good thoughts are the only power.

SEE the following stories:

- "Jairus' Daughter Brought Back to Life," p. 69
- "Woman Healed of Illness," p. 76
- "Two Men Healed of Blindness," p. 81

SEE John 8:29.

MATTHEW 10:8

"Heal the sick, cleanse the lepers, raise the dead, cast out devils."

Jesus never doubted that God's children are always loved and cared for by God. He wasn't afraid of what his eyes and ears told him—whether it was sickness, sin, or death. Instead, he knew the truth that God, who is Spirit, keeps us all just the way we are made by God—in the image and likeness of Spirit. Jesus knew that since God's children reflect good, they can't help but be good and healthy all the time.

Jesus expected his disciples to heal, too. He taught them how. And they were good students—they healed people of sickness and sin and brought people back to life by knowing the truths Jesus knew. We're also disciples, or students. We can heal others, too!

What can YOU do?

Does reading about how Jesus made people happy by healing them make you want to do that, too? You can! Try to think and act the way Jesus did. Jesus loved God with all his heart, and he loved everyone else, too. He loved *God* by knowing God is everywhere and the only power. So, there isn't any room for bad thoughts of sickness or sadness. Jesus loved *everyone else* by seeing them as God's children, spiritual and perfect. This is the love that heals. When you love others and want to be helpful just as Jesus was, you'll find ways to heal wherever you are. God will be right there giving you just the ideas you need.

Read a testimony related to this healing on page 250, "Speech Difficulty Healed."

Jesus destroyed the demon, or bad thought, in an instant by knowing what was true. And when the bad thought was destroyed, the man could speak!

Think what it meant for him to be able to talk to others. He didn't have to be silent anymore. He must have left that house shouting with joy!

When the crowd knew that Jesus had healed this man, they were amazed. Everyone was saying, "Healings like this have never been seen among the Jews!" ∎

MAN HEALED OF DISABILITY

One time when Jesus went to Jerusalem during one of the **festivals**, he walked to a place called the Pool of Bethesda. Many people who were sick or blind or couldn't walk were sitting or lying on the porches around the pool.

This was a large pool, probably about the size of a football field. It had covered porches on four sides and a fifth porch down the center that divided the pool into two parts.

To find more information on color-coded terms, see pages 261–282.

CONCEPTS CUSTOMS GLOSSARY PEOPLE PLACES

87

People believed the water had special power to heal—but only when it was moving. And it moved only at certain times. People thought that the first person to step into the water when it started bubbling would be healed. So everyone hoped to be the first one in. But Jesus saw a man there who didn't look very hopeful.

This man had not been able to walk for 38 years. When Jesus saw the man, he didn't have to ask him if he had been there a long time. He knew it. Jesus listened for God's thoughts, so he knew people's needs. He said to the man, "Do you want to be well?"

The man replied, "Sir, when the water moves, I don't have a friend to put me into the pool. While I'm trying to get to the water, someone else always steps in before me."

Jesus told the man to do something that probably seemed impossible for someone who hadn't walked for a long time. He said firmly, "Rise, pick up your bed, and walk." Jesus did not believe this man was weak and unable to walk. Instead, he knew that this man's true nature was spiritual and that he was God's child, strong and able to be active.

Jesus may have asked the man if he wanted to be well in order to help him think about whether he *really* wanted to be healed. Since this man had been unable to walk for so long, he might have gotten into the habit of not being able to take care of himself and of having others feel sorry for him. He may even have lost all hope that he could ever be healed. Jesus might have wanted to break the man's habit of feeling helpless and hopeless. Maybe Jesus asked the man whether he wanted to be healed in order to awaken **faith** in the man—to help him *expect* to be healed.

SEE Sabbath Laws, p. 269.

The man felt the power of Jesus' command, and he was changed immediately. He stood up and walked away, carrying his bed on his shoulder. He must have been so happy to walk after all those years!

But some other people were not so happy about the healing.

Several of the Jews, seeing this man carrying his bed, said to him, "This is the Sabbath day. It is against the law for you to carry your bed today."

The man answered, "The man who healed me told me to pick up my bed and walk."

The Jews asked him, "Who told you to take up your bed and walk?" But the man didn't know Jesus' name, and he couldn't find him because Jesus had disappeared into the crowd.

The man then went to the Temple. This was the most important place in the world for Jews to worship God.

SEE **Laws of Cleanness**, p. 268.

ISAIAH 40:31

"They that wait upon the Lord shall renew their strength; . . . they shall run, and not be weary; and they shall walk, and not faint."

Jesus helped this man trust God's goodness and power. He helped the man see that he could be free of the fear that he couldn't move like other people. When Jesus commanded him to get up, carry his bed, and walk, the man knew instantly that he could do it. He felt the energy of Spirit. God doesn't make us weak. God makes us perfect and strong. Jesus knew this and proved it. And we can, too.

When the man had been disabled and couldn't move quickly, people believed he was "unclean." Because of this, he had not been allowed to go to the Temple—that was the law. But now that

he was well, he could go in. Imagine how good it must have felt to worship God in the Temple for the first time in many years!

Jesus went to the Temple, too. He found the man there and said to him, "Think about it! You have been healed. From now on, don't sin, because something worse may happen to you." Jesus was telling this man how important it is to listen to God and do what's right in order to stay well and happy.

The man left the Temple and told the Jewish leaders that Jesus was the man who had healed him. He loved sharing the good news! ▪

What can YOU do?

Have you ever felt that you needed a friend to talk to or to help you? You can know that God is your friend who always loves you. You can look for good everywhere you are. Every time you see something good in your life—even the tiniest thing—that's a peek at God's great love for you. The more carefully you look, the more good you'll see and feel, because God's goodness is everywhere. And you'll find that you have whatever help you need. You'll also find yourself loving others more and being a friend to them!

MATTHEW 15:21–28

WOMAN'S DAUGHTER HEALED OF ILLNESS

You can find another account of this healing in Mark 7:24–30.

Jesus had been in Jerusalem, where he healed a man who had been disabled for 38 years.  When he returned home to Galilee, people brought him many who were sick, and he healed them, too.

One day Jesus left Galilee with his disciples and traveled to Phoenicia, where many Gentiles lived. Most Gentiles didn't believe in the one God, but many of them from this area had gone to Galilee to hear Jesus and be healed.

SEE "Man Healed of Disability," p. 87.

Mark says that Jesus "entered into an house, and would have no man know it" (Mark 7:24). It was probably the home of a Gentile. If so, Jesus was breaking one of the Jewish **laws of cleanness** by going into the house.

To find more information on color-coded terms, see pages 261–282.

CONCEPTS   CUSTOMS   GLOSSARY   PEOPLE   PLACES

Jesus taught and healed many people from **Phoenicia**. He spoke of their **faith** and willingness to learn. (See Mark 3:8; Luke 6:17–19; Luke 10:13.)

Jesus spent most of his time in **Palestine**, teaching and healing his fellow Jews, but he also went to areas where Gentiles lived, such as **Samaria**, **Decapolis**, Caesarea Philippi, and Phoenicia. And Gentiles came to hear him and to be healed. Jesus expected his disciples to teach and heal all kinds of people, too. He told them to go and "teach all nations" (Matthew 28:19).

A woman there, who knew about Jesus and his healings, followed him, begging for help. This woman was very brave to talk to Jesus. In Bible times, women weren't supposed to talk to men in public, but she called out to him, "Have mercy on me, O Lord, Son of David!" This name means "Messiah," or "Christ," a name the Jews used for a special king or prophet they believed would come one day to help and heal them. By calling Jesus this, the woman may have been showing him that she had **faith** he could help her. Next, she said, "My daughter has a **demon** in her that is making her very sick."

Matthew describes her as "a woman of Canaan" (Matthew 15:22). Mark says she was "a Greek, a Syrophenician by nation" (Mark 7:26). They both make it clear that her background, culture, language, and religion were very different from that of Jesus.

In those days, everybody—Gentiles and Jews—believed invisible beings called demons could get inside people and make them sick and confused. But Jesus knew that the only power anywhere is God's power of good. So, he knew that there are no such things as

 SEE other examples of Jesus healing Gentiles:

- "Centurion's Servant Healed of Paralysis," p. 41
- "Man Healed of Mental Illness (Gadara)," p. 59

Jesus said he was sent to "the lost sheep of the house of Israel" (Matthew 15:24). "House of Israel" meant "Jews." "The lost sheep" could have had two different meanings:

- The *Am-Ha-Aretz*. These were the common country people who were looked down on by the Pharisees and scribes because they ignored their ritual laws.
- The whole Jewish nation. Prophets had told of a **Messiah** who would be like a shepherd to the Jews (see Ezekiel 34:11, 23). Jesus may have meant he was sent first to the Jews, who were expecting such a shepherd.

demons and that there is no evil power that can make people sick or mixed up. Jesus knew that God loved the woman's daughter and had made her healthy and good.

Jesus didn't answer the woman right away. He may have been testing his disciples to see what they would do. Jesus had taught his disciples the importance of loving others. But they weren't being very loving to this woman. Instead, they said to Jesus, "Send her away. She keeps following us and calling out." But Jesus didn't send the woman away. His purpose was to help people—both Jews and Gentiles.

Jesus said to the disciples, "I've been sent to the Jews who are like lost sheep." Jesus might have been saying that his mission was to help those Jews who were meek and were willing to follow him the way sheep listen to and follow their shepherd. Although

this woman was a Gentile, she, too, was meek and ready to listen to Jesus' words.

She fell down at Jesus' feet and begged him, "Lord, help me!" Because Jesus listened closely to God, he already knew how much this mother loved her daughter and wanted her to be healed. And he could see that this woman had faith that he could heal her child. He could also tell that she wasn't going to give up on getting help for her daughter.

Both Jesus and the woman knew that his disciples didn't think Jesus should help her because she was a Gentile. So he said out loud what his disciples might have been thinking. He said, "It isn't right to take the children's bread and give it to dogs." Here, the word "children" meant the Jews. "Bread" meant God's goodness,

GALATIANS 3:28

"There is neither Jew nor Greek, there is neither bond nor free, there is neither male nor female: for ye are all one in Christ Jesus."

Jesus knew that God, Spirit, is the only creator. This means that everyone God has created is spiritual and good. It doesn't matter whether people are Jewish or Greek, enslaved or free, male or female—God sees them as spiritual. That's also how Jesus saw people. And he knew that God loves everyone equally—no one is left out. Because of that, no matter who needed healing, Jesus was ready to help—to see God's healing power right at hand. Like Jesus, we can know that everyone is created and loved equally by God. As we follow Christ Jesus' example, we'll be willing to help anyone who needs healing. We'll also be helping to bring peace to the world.

SEE **Laws of Cleanness**, p. 268.

Jesus was pleased by the woman's response. She not only had great faith but also was able to express herself in a delightful way, using the same ideas Jesus had used—children, dogs, and bread.

The Bible records Jesus praising only one other person for having great faith. This was the Roman centurion—who was also a Gentile (see Matthew 8:10; Luke 7:9). See also "Centurion's Servant Healed of Paralysis," p. 41.

Read a testimony related to this healing on page 240, "A Daughter's Healing."

love, and healing power. And "dogs" meant the Gentiles. Jews sometimes called Gentiles "dogs" because they thought Gentiles were unclean—like dogs.

Would the woman give a good answer to show the disciples that she deserved his help?

Yes, she had a great answer! She said, "It's true, Lord, but the dogs eat the crumbs that fall from their master's table." This was a way of showing how desperately she wanted help for her daughter. And she was saying that in God's family, there is enough love to heal everyone—the children and the dogs. The Jews *and* the Gentiles!

Jesus certainly knew that, too. He knew that God created everything and everyone and that God cares for all, forever. God doesn't have favorites and give more good to some people than to others. As divine Love, God loves all equally. Jews and Gentiles. Men and women. Girls and boys.

Jesus answered the woman with joy: "O woman! You have great faith!" He could see how much she trusted in God's goodness.

There was a lesson for the disciples in what Jesus said, too. They needed to realize that this Gentile woman had strong faith and deserved his help.

Then Jesus said what she wanted so much to hear.

Mark tells us that Jesus said, "For this saying go thy way; the devil is gone out of thy daughter" (Mark 7:29).

Mark also tells us that the woman went to her house and "found the devil gone out, and her daughter laid upon the bed" (Mark 7:30). Her daughter was completely free of her illness and was resting on her bed.

What can YOU do?

He told her, "What you wanted has happened." And at that very moment, her daughter was completely well. Jesus had never believed the lie that she was sick. He knew the truth that God, who is all-powerful, was always taking care of her. And this truth healed her, even though she was someplace else.

This woman knew her daughter had been healed. She had believed and trusted that there was a God who could heal. She had made the effort to find Jesus, the man who understood God's healing love better than anyone else. She had expected healing and had not given up, trusting in God and expecting good.

What a great day—for the woman, her daughter, and the disciples, who learned that God's love and healing power are always right at hand for everyone!

Sometimes when you need to be healed, you might get discouraged. Maybe you think you aren't good enough to be healed or your problem is too hard or you feel far away from God. All these thoughts are lies. You don't have to believe them. The woman in this story didn't listen to any of these lies. She expected her daughter to be healed. And so did Jesus. He knew all God's children are completely loved by God. And he knew God's healing presence is everywhere and all-powerful. God is right where you are and loves you more than you can even imagine. You can expect healing, too!

MAN HEALED OF DEAFNESS AND SPEECH PROBLEMS

Jesus had been in Phoenicia, where he healed the daughter of a Gentile woman.

Instead of going back to his own country, Galilee, he crossed the Jordan River and traveled to Decapolis. Large crowds followed him. Most of the people there were Gentiles, and many had heard of Jesus.

To find more information on color-coded terms, see pages 261–282.

CONCEPTS | CUSTOMS | GLOSSARY | PEOPLE | PLACES

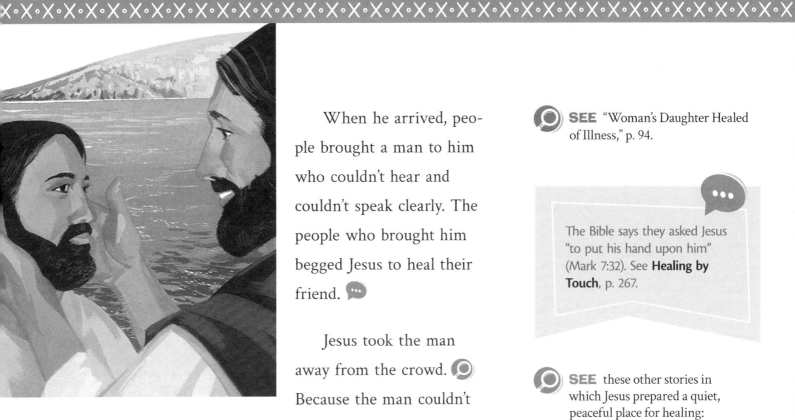

When he arrived, people brought a man to him who couldn't hear and couldn't speak clearly. The people who brought him begged Jesus to heal their friend.

Jesus took the man away from the crowd. Because the man couldn't hear, Jesus used a kind of sign language to explain that he would heal him. First, Jesus touched the man's ears to show him that he would be healed of deafness. Next, he touched the man's tongue to show him that he would be healed of his speech problems.

Then, Jesus looked up to the sky. This was another signal to help the man have better and higher thoughts—to look away from his problem and think about God as the healing power. When people looked up as Jesus did, it was a way of saying that they were listening to God. This man might have been a Gentile who believed in many different gods. But Jesus wanted him to have **faith** that there is only one God, who is good, all-powerful, and everywhere.

SEE "Woman's Daughter Healed of Illness," p. 94.

The Bible says they asked Jesus "to put his hand upon him" (Mark 7:32). See **Healing by Touch**, p. 267.

SEE these other stories in which Jesus prepared a quiet, peaceful place for healing:

- "Jairus' Daughter Brought Back to Life," p. 69

- "Two Men Healed of Blindness," p. 81

- "Man Healed of Blindness," p. 104

Here, the Bible says that Jesus "spit, and touched his tongue" (Mark 7:33). See **Spit**, p. 269.

DEUTERONOMY 30:14

"The word is very nigh unto thee, in thy mouth, and in thy heart, that thou mayest do it."

God's word—God's messages of love and truth—are as close as the words in our mouths or the thoughts in our hearts. As we listen to God and are grateful for God's great goodness, we'll hear what will bless us and others. When Jesus met people who couldn't hear or speak, he didn't believe this was true about them. He knew everyone's true nature reflects God's perfection. Understanding this allows us to hear and speak perfectly. Jesus showed that listening to God's messages and knowing what's true brings healing. As we listen to these messages, we, too, will hear God telling us what to know and what to say, and this will bring healing to others as well as ourselves.

The Bible tells us that Jesus said, "*Ephphatha*," which means "be opened" in Aramaic, the language Jesus spoke (Mark 7:34).

Next, Jesus breathed a deep sigh. This may have been a way for Jesus to show the man that he was listening with all his might to God and God's messages of love and healing.

Then Jesus spoke to the man for the first time. He gave this command: "Be opened!"

Jesus expected the man to hear, understand, and obey this order. He knew that since God is Spirit and all-powerful, God's children are spiritual, perfect, and free. He knew that nothing could keep this man from being free.

The instant that Jesus said, "Be opened," the man was healed! Not only did the man hear, but he began to speak clearly, too.

Then, Jesus ordered the people, "**Don't tell anyone** about the healing."

But the man who was healed and the people nearby were so amazed that they couldn't help telling others. Even though Jesus kept telling them to be quiet, the man and his friends told many people about it.

Everyone who heard the story was amazed. They all said, "Jesus can do everything and do it perfectly. He can make the deaf hear and the mute speak." ■

What can YOU do?

Maybe someone you know is hard to talk to because he or she has a disability. Jesus found ways to talk to this man who couldn't hear or speak. Jesus used a kind of sign language to tell the man he would heal him. When you love others the way Jesus loved, you can find just the right way to let them know you love them and want to help them.

God wants you to love others and be a friend to them. If you turn to God as Jesus did, you'll find God is showing you lots of ways to love.

Read a testimony related to this healing on page 252, "Daughter's Normal Hearing Restored."

MARK 8:22–26

MAN HEALED OF BLINDNESS

After healing a man of deafness and speech problems, Jesus traveled to Bethsaida.  Even though he was well-known in Bethsaida because he had healed many there, most people in the town didn't really listen to Jesus or follow him. 💬

But a few paid attention to his healings, and some of them brought a blind man to Jesus and begged him to help the man. 💬 The first thing Jesus did was take the blind man by the hand and lead him out of the town. Jesus must have wanted to be alone with the man and away from the people of Bethsaida who had so little **faith** in his healing power. 🔍

🔍 **SEE** "Man Healed of Deafness and Speech Problems," p. 100.

💬 Bethsaida was one of the cities where many of Jesus' healings took place. But Jesus rebuked the people there for not changing their thinking after seeing his mighty healing works (see Matthew 11:20–21).

💬 The Bible says they "besought him to touch him" (Mark 8:22). See **Healing by Touch**, p. 267.

To find more information on color-coded terms, see pages 261–282.

CONCEPTS · CUSTOMS · GLOSSARY · PEOPLE · PLACES

Once they were away from the town, Jesus touched the man's eyes to show him that he would be healed. Then, Jesus put his hands on him to comfort him.

Next, Jesus asked him if he saw anything. The man looked and said, "I can see people, but they look like trees walking around." The man could see a little, but he wasn't completely healed.

Jesus knew that God's healing power didn't stop when someone got a little better. So Jesus kept knowing what was true about the man—that it was natural for a child of God to express God perfectly. Then, he touched the man's eyes again to let him know he was still with him and praying—and to encourage him to keep expecting good. Jesus also made the man look up to help him look away from his problem and think about God.

The man opened his eyes and looked again, and this time he was able to see clearly. What a great feeling that must have been!

SEE these other stories in which Jesus prepared a quiet, peaceful place for healing:

- "Jairus' Daughter Brought Back to Life," p. 69
- "Two Men Healed of Blindness," p. 81
- "Man Healed of Deafness and Speech Problems," p. 100

Here, the Bible says that Jesus "spit on his eyes, and put his hands upon him" (Mark 8:23). See **Spit**, p. 269, and **Healing by Touch**, p. 267.

What can YOU do?

Sometimes when you pray, you may feel your prayers aren't answered right away. Or you may only get part of the answer. You may even lose hope and think your prayers have failed. But prayer is a lot like working on a project at school. You need to keep working on it until it's finished.

Jesus showed the blind man that he should keep expecting to be healed. You can do that, too. Keep praying. Keep listening to God's angel messages. God loves you and gives you only good. God's guidance and healing power never stop. When you keep trusting God's love and listening for God's messages, you will learn wonderful new things about God and about yourself. And you will find complete healing.

Jesus knew that God's children are always perfect and that understanding this brings complete healing. When this man's eyesight improved but wasn't completely clear, Jesus didn't give up. And he wouldn't let the man give up either. Jesus turned to God in prayer for healing. And he knew God doesn't answer prayer halfway. No matter what the man said was wrong with his eyes, Jesus stayed firm, knowing that God keeps everyone perfect in every way.

Jesus knew that if he shut out of his thinking any lies about this man and kept his thought filled with what was true about him, they would both see the results of his prayer—and they did. Each of us has the same ability to be steadfast. We can hold on to the truth, just as Jesus did, no matter what. And we'll find healing, too.

He must have been so grateful that Jesus hadn't given up on healing him!

Jesus then told the man, "Go straight home. Don't go into the town. And **don't tell anyone** from town about your healing."

Maybe Jesus felt that most people in Bethsaida had so little faith in God's healing power that they might question the man and argue with him. Jesus wouldn't have wanted the man to go through that. Instead, Jesus probably wanted him to have some quiet time to think about his healing and be grateful for his new faith in God's power. ■

MATTHEW 17:14–21

MAN'S SON HEALED OF EPILEPSY

You can find other accounts of this healing in Mark 9:17–29 and Luke 9:37–42.

After healing a blind man near Bethsaida,  Jesus led his disciples to a mountain. While nine of the disciples waited at the bottom of the mountain, Jesus took Peter, James, and John up with him to teach them important lessons.

When Jesus and the three disciples came down, a man who was very worried about his son saw Jesus and went to him. The man kneeled at Jesus' feet and begged him for help. He said, "Lord, have

To find more information on color-coded terms, see pages 261–282.

NCEPTS | CUSTOMS | GLOSSARY | PEOPLE | PLACES

SEE "Man Healed of Blindness," p. 104.

This could have been Mount Hermon, the highest mountain in Palestine. Its snow-covered peaks can be seen for many miles.

Luke says this was the man's only child (see Luke 9:38).

107

mercy on my son! Often, he is wild and falls into the fire or the water and hurts himself." People believed that invisible beings called **demons** could get inside people and make them sick or wild. But Jesus knew that demons were only wrong thoughts, or lies. He knew that God is the only power and destroys these lies.

The father said, "I brought him to your disciples, but they couldn't heal him."

The father, the disciples, and the crowd all waited to hear what Jesus would say. He spoke strong words, which were probably meant for the disciples. He said, "How little faith you have! You've turned away from what you learned—that God is the only power! How long will I have to be with you before you understand? How much longer do I have to be patient with you?"

The disciples had heard Jesus talk about God's power so many times and seen so many wonderful healings. He wanted them—and everyone else—to understand that it is natural to heal when you have complete **faith** in God. He wanted them to understand that nothing is impossible to God.

Jesus then said to the father, "Bring your son to me."

Jesus' faith was strong and constant. He knew that everyone is given only good from God—because God is good. This boy's sickness wasn't good. God hadn't created it and wouldn't allow it, so it had no power.

When the boy was brought to him, Jesus spoke firmly to the demon, or wrong thought. And the boy was healed—right then!

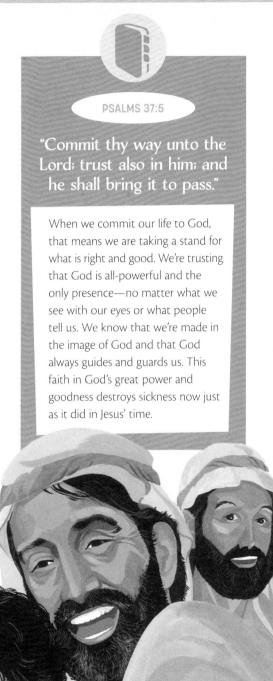

PSALMS 37:5

"Commit thy way unto the Lord; trust also in him; and he shall bring it to pass."

When we commit our life to God, that means we are taking a stand for what is right and good. We're trusting that God is all-powerful and the only presence—no matter what we see with our eyes or what people tell us. We know that we're made in the image of God and that God always guides and guards us. This faith in God's great power and goodness destroys sickness now just as it did in Jesus' time.

109

How thankful and happy the boy's father must have been to see his son completely well!

Afterward, the disciples stepped away from the crowd and spoke to Jesus. They asked him why they hadn't been able to heal the boy. Jesus said to them, "Because you didn't have faith. You didn't trust that God is the only power."

Then he explained that even a little faith is very powerful. He said, "If you have faith even as small as a mustard seed, you'll be able to do great things. You can tell a mountain to move to another place, and it will happen. Nothing will be impossible to you." When Jesus told them they could move mountains, it was like saying they could heal any problem if they had faith.

The disciples were probably glad to hear that even a little faith in God is powerful. Their teacher had given them another great lesson to help them become better healers.

Here, Matthew and Mark say that Jesus continued his discussion with his disciples (see Matthew 17:19–21; Mark 9:28–29). He told them that cases like this could be healed only by "prayer and fasting." "Fasting" can mean "not eating." During Jesus' time, Jews fasted for various reasons—at someone's death, before a war, and on special occasions such as the Day of Atonement. But when he told his disciples that they could heal this boy only by prayer and fasting, he meant "fasting" in a deeper way. He meant they should not take into their thought the scary things they saw with their eyes. Instead, they needed to pray—to let their thought be filled with God's power and love for this boy. Some translations of the Bible don't even have the word "fasting"—only "prayer."

What can YOU do?

When someone you know is sick, you may be tempted to be afraid or to believe that God can't help that person. Jesus told his disciples to have faith—to trust in God's all-power. He knew that with even a little faith a person can do what seems impossible. He told his disciples that if they had faith even as small as a mustard seed (which is tiny), it would be enough to do great things. Faith in God means keeping your thought on God's wonderful love and great power. With this kind of faith, you can see that sickness is not a big, impossible thing to heal. Nothing is too hard for God.

Read a testimony related to this healing on page 243, "Epilepsy Healed."

LUKE 13:10–17

WOMAN HEALED OF BACK PROBLEM

After Jesus healed a boy of epilepsy near Mount Hermon,  he headed toward Jerusalem. Along the way, he taught and preached in the towns and countryside of Galilee.

This mountain is in northern **Palestine** and is the highest mountain in the region (9,100 feet or 2,774 meters).

SEE "Man's Son Healed of Epilepsy," p. 107.

To find more information on color-coded terms, see pages 261–282.

| CONCEPTS | CUSTOMS | GLOSSARY | PEOPLE | PLACES |

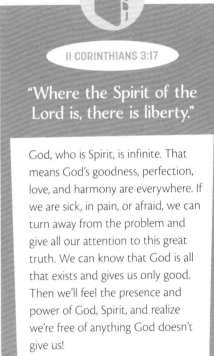

II CORINTHIANS 3:17

"Where the Spirit of the Lord is, there is liberty."

God, who is Spirit, is infinite. That means God's goodness, perfection, love, and harmony are everywhere. If we are sick, in pain, or afraid, we can turn away from the problem and give all our attention to this great truth. We can know that God is all that exists and gives us only good. Then we'll feel the presence and power of God, Spirit, and realize we're free of anything God doesn't give us!

Wherever Jesus went, he visited synagogues and often taught in them on the Sabbath day.

One Sabbath, while Jesus was teaching, he saw a woman who was bent over and couldn't stand up straight. She had been that way for a very long time—18 years.

When Jesus saw the woman, he called her over to him and said, "You are free!" She or others may have thought that she was bent over because an evil spirit was hurting her. 🔍 But Jesus knew that nothing could keep her from being able to stand up straight. He knew that evil spirits weren't real. They were only bad thoughts that had no power over this woman—or anyone.

He knew she was free of the evil thought that something could make her stay bent over. God, who is the only Spirit, had created her, so she was God's child—always spiritual, perfect, and well. And since God is the only power, there couldn't be any evil power to make her sick or in pain or bent over.

SEE Demon, p. 263.

SEE Healing by Touch, p. 267.

When Jesus told the woman, "You are free," he was telling her that she was healed.

Jesus then reached out and touched the woman, which must have made her feel very happy and loved.  And she was healed immediately—right away, she stood up straight!

Can you imagine how grateful she was to be able to walk normally? She showed everyone how thankful she was by saying to Jesus and the people in the synagogue that God is great and powerful. She was brave to speak out like that!

115

SEE Exodus 20:8.

But the ruler of the synagogue was angry about this wonderful healing.

He believed Jesus had broken the Fourth Commandment, which says the Sabbath should be kept holy. Jews believed that people should rest on the Sabbath day.

The Jewish leaders had created **Sabbath laws** listing what kind of work was allowed and what kind was not allowed on the Sabbath. They said that healing was not allowed unless the sickness was very bad.

The ruler of the synagogue thought Jesus should have waited until the Sabbath was over to heal this woman. He told everyone, "There are six days when people can work.

116

Come and be healed on *those* days—not on the Sabbath."

Jesus disagreed. He asked, "Doesn't each of you on the Sabbath day untie your ox or your donkey and set it free from the barn so you can lead it to water? Then shouldn't this daughter of Abraham, who hasn't been able to stand up straight for 18 years, be set free— be healed—on the Sabbath day?"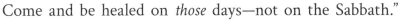

Jesus knew it was always right to heal—no matter what day it was—because healing expresses God's goodness by showing love for others. He was pointing out that the ruler and those who believed

Jesus described the woman's problem as being bound by "Satan" (Luke 13:16). This term is used in the Bible to mean "evil"—that which is the opposite of God. Jesus once said about Satan or the Devil that "there is no truth in him" and that "he is a liar, and the father of it" (John 8:44). Jesus knew that God is everywhere and all-powerful and that this truth had freed the woman from believing in any other power.

Standing up for what is right may seem hard to do sometimes—especially when those around you don't agree with you. But you can know, as Jesus did when he stood up for the woman, that your Father-Mother God loves you and will help you. God gives you the right words to say and keeps you safe. You can be strong and unafraid, knowing that God is always right there with you.

Read a testimony related to this healing on page 251, "Healed of Back Pain."

him *said* they loved God and wanted to help people but *showed* more love for their animals than for people. If they had really loved others, they would have been happy about this healing and would have praised God.

What Jesus said made the ruler and those who agreed with him feel ashamed. Everyone else now understood that what the ruler had said about not healing on the Sabbath day wasn't right at all. And they were very happy about all of Jesus' wonderful healings! ■

LUKE 14:1–6

MAN HEALED OF SWELLING

After Jesus healed a woman who couldn't stand up straight, he continued traveling to Jerusalem.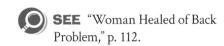

◉ SEE "Woman Healed of Back Problem," p. 112.

On the way, a leader of the Pharisees invited him to dinner at his house. The leader and his guests were all watching Jesus because it was the Sabbath day.

The leader's guests were other Pharisees and scribes, who were also called lawyers. They may have heard that Jesus healed people on the

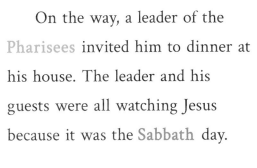

To find more information on color-coded terms, see pages 261–282.

| CONCEPTS | CUSTOMS | GLOSSARY | PEOPLE | PLACES |

SEE the following stories where Jesus heals on the Sabbath day:

- "Man Healed of Mental Illness (Capernaum)," p. 14

- "Man with Withered Hand Healed," p. 32

- "Man Healed of Disability," p. 87

- "Woman Healed of Back Problem," p. 112

 **SEE** Exodus 20:8.

Sabbath day.  They thought this broke the Fourth Commandment—"Remember the sabbath day, to keep it holy." But Jesus knew that doing good works through God's power is a perfect way to keep the Sabbath holy.

The Jewish leaders had made **Sabbath laws** that listed what kind of work people could do on the Sabbath and what kind they weren't allowed to do. They believed that healing was work and that it shouldn't be done on the Sabbath unless the sickness was so bad that it couldn't wait until later to be cured.

DEUTERONOMY 31:6

"Be strong and of a good courage, fear not, nor be afraid of them: for the Lord thy God, he it is that doth go with thee; he will not fail thee, nor forsake thee."

Jesus knew that God was always with him, always showing him the best thing to say or do. So when others were unkind or angry with him, Jesus wasn't afraid. He knew he could go ahead and do what God was telling him to do because God, who is all-powerful, was right there with him, keeping him safe. Jesus' example helps us see that God is always with us, too. So, if we are sick or someone is angry with us, we don't have to be afraid. We can know that God is in control.

The Pharisees and scribes may have been watching to see whether Jesus would heal anyone because they wanted to accuse him of breaking a Sabbath law. That way, they might be able to get rid of him, and then the people would follow *them*, instead of Jesus. They didn't have to wait long to see what would happen, because right in front of Jesus was a man who needed to be healed.

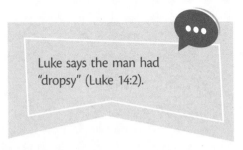

Luke says the man had "dropsy" (Luke 14:2).

 SEE Healing by Touch, p. 267.

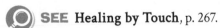

Here the Bible uses the word "ass" for "donkey" (Luke 14:5). However, many early manuscripts say "son."

The Jewish laws allowed certain types of work to be done on the **Sabbath**. It was okay to pull a child or an animal out of a hole dug in the ground (like a pit or a well). But these laws did not allow healing on the Sabbath unless the person was expected to die.

This man had a sickness that made his body swollen.

Jesus surprised the Pharisees and scribes by asking them the very thing they were thinking about. He said, "Does the law allow healing on the Sabbath day?" The Pharisees just sat there and didn't answer Jesus.

Next, Jesus reached out and touched the man who was sick. That probably made him feel very loved. Jesus knew that God had created this man—and all of God's children—spiritual and perfect. And he knew that God keeps everyone perfect, so there is no place for sickness. Jesus understood that God loves everyone and takes care of them, and God doesn't allow anything bad to happen to them.

That understanding healed the man instantly! Think how happy he was to be free of this sickness!

After Jesus healed the man, he sent him on his way. He might have done this so the man wouldn't have to answer questions from the Pharisees and scribes about being healed on the Sabbath.

But Jesus loved everyone, even the Pharisees. So he turned to them and asked them another question. "If your donkey or your ox fell into a well on the Sabbath, wouldn't you pull him out right away?" Jesus knew that all of them would help their animals.

What can YOU do?

When you know it's right to do something, you can be brave and do it. Just as Jesus had to stand up to the Jewish leaders who were angry with him, you can listen to God and do what God tells you to do, even if that means standing up to someone who tries to stop you from doing good. God loves you and gives you the strength to do whatever you need to do.

The Pharisees didn't answer him. They couldn't answer because if they admitted that they would help their ox on the Sabbath, they would have to admit that healing this man was the loving thing to do on the Sabbath. They realized that what Jesus had done was right. Loving and helping others is always right!

TEN MEN HEALED OF LEPROSY

 **SEE** the following stories:

- "Woman Healed of Back Problem," p. 112
- "Man Healed of Swelling," p. 119

As Jesus was traveling from Galilee to Jerusalem, he stopped along the way to teach and heal. In one of the places he stopped, he healed a woman who couldn't stand up straight, and in another place he healed a man whose body was very swollen.

On this day, he was going through the land of Samaria. Usually, Jews didn't travel in Samaria because Jews and Samaritans didn't get along with each other. But Jesus loved all people. He knew they were all children of God, who is the Father and Mother of everyone.

To find more information on color-coded terms, see pages 261–282.

CONCEPTS CUSTOMS GLOSSARY PEOPLE PLACES

As Jesus was going into a town, ten lepers outside the city gate were coming toward him. They were called "lepers" because they had leprosy, a kind of sickness that made their skin look bad.

SEE "Man Healed of Leprosy," p. 22.

Jewish **laws of cleanness** said that anyone with leprosy had to stay away from other people. The laws also said that lepers were supposed to call out, "Unclean! Unclean!" to warn people to stay away from them. But when the lepers saw Jesus, they shouted something else instead.

They called out, "Jesus, Master, have mercy on us!"

Perhaps they had heard that Jesus was very kind and that he had healed people, including another leper. By asking for mercy, the lepers were asking Jesus to show love and tenderness by healing them.

Did Jesus turn away from the lepers?

"Be ye therefore perfect, even as your Father which is in heaven is perfect."

It's wonderful to know what's true about God and God's children! Everyone is created by God in the image and likeness of God. That means we are all God's spiritual reflections—perfect, just as God is perfect. Jesus knew that since God's children are perfect, sickness is never a part of them. Everyone's true nature reflects God and is always healthy. This powerful truth heals people. We can know what's true and heal just as Jesus did.

Of course not! He was ready to answer their call for help. Jesus knew that God, good, is the only power. He wasn't bothered by the way the lepers' skin looked. He saw them as God's children, created in God's image and likeness—perfect, pure, loved, and always cared for by God.

Jesus said to the men, "Go and show yourselves to the priests." This was like saying the lepers were already healed because lepers wouldn't go to a priest unless they thought they were healed. The law said that a priest had to look at the lepers' skin carefully. If the priest said the men were healed, they could go back home and live like everyone else.

SEE **Purification Rituals**, p. 269.

Right away, the lepers obeyed Jesus and headed off to see the priests. Their skin didn't look any different yet, but they had **faith** that Jesus would heal them.

And he did. As the men were walking away, they were all healed. They must have been really happy about this amazing healing! Maybe they thought about how their lives would change and how they could be with their families and friends again.

Then one of the men stopped and turned back. In a very loud voice, he shouted about God's goodness and about how thankful he was to be healed.

Next, he went to Jesus and threw himself on the ground in front of him and thanked him. This was surprising because the man wasn't a Jew. He was a Samaritan—and Samaritans didn't usually get close to Jews.

What can YOU do?

Being grateful for all the ways (both little and big) that God loves you and takes care of you is powerful! When your thoughts are filled with God's goodness, there's no room for bad thoughts—for worries or fears. Giving thanks to God is a great way to keep your thought focused on divine Love. Thanking God makes you happy and helps you understand that God has created you—and everyone—perfect. Each day you can find wonderful ways that God loves you and everyone. You'll probably find more ways than you can count! Your thanksgiving will bless you and the whole world.

Read a testimony related to this healing on page 257, "Rash Healed."

Jesus said, "Weren't ten men healed? Why is this Samaritan the only one who turned back to give thanks to God?" Giving thanks to God helps people feel God's love. It also helps them remember God's goodness long after they're healed.

Jesus then told the man, "Get up and go on your way! Your faith has made you completely well." Jesus knew that trust in God is important in healing, and he wanted the man to know that, too. He hoped the man understood that faith in God had healed him. ∎

JOHN 8:1–11

WOMAN HEALED OF ADULTERY

Jesus traveled to the Temple in Jerusalem. There, people crowded around him to hear him teach. Some thought he was the **Messiah**—a special king they believed God would send to help and heal them.

The scribes and Pharisees in Jerusalem weren't happy because the people were listening to Jesus instead of to them.

To find more information on color-coded terms, see pages 261–282.

CONCEPTS CUSTOMS GLOSSARY PEOPLE PLACES

JOHN 7:24

"Judge not according to the appearance, but judge righteous judgment."

Jesus knew that the right way to judge people is to see them the way God sees them. The woman who was brought to him appeared to be a sinner, but Jesus judged her the right way. Jesus knew that this woman was created in the image and likeness of God, who is Spirit, so she was really God's spiritual, perfect creation. And he knew that God kept her that way—always. Judging, or seeing, the woman this way protected her from the men who wanted to stone her and helped her do what was right from then on. Seeing others as God sees them is a powerful prayer that helps people feel better and act better.

They argued with Jesus and even tried to have him arrested. In the evening, Jesus went to the Mount of Olives to spend the night. This was a high hill across a valley from Jerusalem. The hill was covered with olive trees. Jesus was probably praying most of the night, feeling God's goodness and power right there with him.

As soon as the sun came up, he was back in the Temple teaching again.

Suddenly, some scribes and Pharisees pushed through the crowd of people listening to Jesus. They had a woman with them,

The Seventh Commandment is "Thou shalt not commit adultery" (Exodus 20:14). People commit adultery if they break their wedding promise and make love to someone they are not married to.

Jewish law stated that *both* the man and the woman who commit adultery should be stoned to death. But in Jesus' time, the law was not completely obeyed. Often only the woman was punished, not the man. If the scribes and Pharisees had fully obeyed the law, they would have brought the man who committed adultery with them as well. In addition, they would have brought two witnesses to prove the couple's guilt. And the guilty man and woman would have been taken to the proper authorities, not to a teacher like Jesus.

and they made her stand in front of Jesus. "Master," they said to him, "this woman was caught committing adultery. The law of Moses says that people who do this should be stoned. What do you say?"

The scribes and Pharisees were trying to trick Jesus. If he said they *shouldn't* stone her, they would say he was disobeying Moses and the Jewish law. But if he said they *should* stone her, he would be going against what he taught about loving others. It seemed that no matter what answer he gave, he would be saying something wrong.

The Bible says that Jesus wrote on the ground "as though he heard them not" (John 8:6). This phrase was added by the translators to the King James Version but does not appear in all Bible translations.

Instead of saying anything, Jesus stooped down and wrote with his finger on the ground.  He must have been praying—listening to God's angel messages to tell him what to do next.

When the scribes and Pharisees kept asking him questions, Jesus stood up and said, "If there is a man here who has never sinned—has never done anything wrong—let him be the first to throw a stone at her." Then he bent down and wrote on the ground again.

When the scribes and Pharisees heard that, they must have thought about their own lives. The oldest man there admitted to himself that he had done things that were wrong. He knew he couldn't throw the first stone. So, without saying a word, he walked away. And one by one, having admitted to themselves that they had also made mistakes, the rest walked away, too.

These men had tried to trick Jesus and make him say something wrong. Instead, they had to face their own wrongs. Jesus was left alone with the woman, who was still standing where the men had left her.

Jesus stood up and saw that everyone except the woman was gone. Then he asked her, "Where are the men who brought you here? Is no one left to call you a sinner and punish you?"

"No one, sir," she replied.

"I don't call you a sinner either," answered Jesus. Jesus didn't call her a sinner because he didn't think of her that way. He knew that God creates everyone pure and good, and this is always true about each of us.

Then Jesus said goodbye with these words: "Go, and sin no more."

Think how grateful this woman must have been! Jesus' kindness and love would have helped her understand that, since she was God's child, she could do what was right from then on. ■

What can YOU do?

If you are ever in a place where people are angry at you, will you be angry back? If they are trying to get you into trouble, will you be upset? Jesus knew that wherever he was and whatever was going on around him, God, his Father-Mother, was right there with him. You can know that, too. Like Jesus, you can calmly turn your thought away from the angry faces and voices. And when your thought is quiet, you'll hear the right ideas you need from God—just as Jesus did. God's ideas tell you exactly what to say or do to help everyone calm down.

MAN HEALED OF BLINDNESS FROM BIRTH

Jesus had been in the Temple in Jerusalem. There, he taught many people and healed a woman of sin. ◉ He also argued with the Jewish leaders. ◉ He told them that God was his Father and that he was "sent" from God. ◉ He meant that he was the Messiah or **Christ** that God had sent to help everyone see the power of God's love in their lives.

To find more information on color-coded terms, see pages 261–282.

| CONCEPTS | CUSTOMS | GLOSSARY | PEOPLE | PLACES |

When Jesus told the Jewish leaders he was sent from God, they didn't believe him and got so angry that they picked up stones to throw at him in order to kill him. But he slipped away from them.

Jesus and his disciples had come to Jerusalem for the **Feast of Tabernacles**. The streets were filled with people, and many beggars were asking for money. Jesus saw one of these beggars—a man who had been born blind. The disciples saw him, too. They turned to Jesus and asked him, "Master, why was this man born blind? Who sinned, the man or his parents? Who did something wrong to make him blind?"

SEE "Woman Healed of Adultery," p. 129.

SEE Scribes, p. 277 and Pharisees, p. 275.

SEE John 8:26–29.

SEE John 8:59.

Most people believed that it was possible to sin before birth. They also thought that if parents sinned, something bad could happen to their children. But Jesus didn't believe this. He told his disciples, "This blindness wasn't caused by sin—not by this man's sin or his parents' sin." Jesus knew that everyone is created in the image and likeness of God, who is all-powerful and completely good. God's creation is good and cannot sin.

Jesus told his disciples, "We're going to see God's work—God's true creation—here."

Then he said, "During the day we must do the works of God, who sent me. At night you won't be able to work." Maybe Jesus was telling his disciples that they had a great opportunity to learn to heal while he was there to teach them. Having him with them was like the daytime, when the sunlight makes it easy to see. When he was gone, it would be like nighttime for a while, when it's dark and hard to see. But then he told them, "I am the **light of the world**." That was a promise that they could continue to heal because Jesus' light was the truth that God's power and love are always with everyone.

136

Next, Jesus did something so the man would know he was going to be healed.

Jesus made some clay and spread it on the man's eyes.  The man had heard Jesus talking to his disciples about how important it is to do God's work. And he must have felt Jesus' kindness and love in his gentle touch. This may have helped the man understand that God's love was right there to heal him.

Jesus didn't think the clay had any power to heal. He knew the thoughts coming to him from God had all the power. Those weren't thoughts about this man being blind. They were about him being God's child, made in God's image, spiritual and perfect.

What would Jesus do next?

He said to the man, "Go and wash in the Pool of Siloam."

Here, the Bible says that Jesus **spit** on the dusty ground, made some clay, and spread it on the eyes of the blind man.

SEE Healing by Touch, p. 267.

"The entrance of thy words giveth light; it giveth understanding unto the simple."

There's nothing better than feeling God's goodness and love! This happens when we open our thought to good and close it to bad. When our thinking is filled with God's good ideas, it's like a room filled with light. No darkness can enter. The light fills all the space, and the darkness has no power and no place to be. In the same way, no dark thoughts about sickness or hurt or sadness or death can have a place in our thinking when it's filled with God's good thoughts. And keeping our thinking filled with good ideas from God brings healing—to us, and to our friends and family, too.

This was a large pool of water in the city. The name, "Siloam," means "sent."

The man went to the pool, washed off the clay, and returned—seeing. For the first time in his life he could see! Imagine how amazed and grateful he must have been to be able to see his family and friends. He could also see with his heart that he and his parents were sinless children of God.

That day the disciples learned not to look for a cause for sickness or disability, because God is the only cause and God's creation is all good. Instead, they learned to see this true creation even where there seemed to be a problem. This lesson helped them do God's work and become better healers. ■

What can YOU do?

Many people believe that sickness, disabilities, and even bad behavior are inherited—that parents can pass along these problems to their children when they're born. Jesus didn't believe that the man's blindness came from his parents or from anything the man had done wrong. You can know, just as Jesus did, that the only real Parent anyone has is God. Your Father-Mother God gives only good—everything you need to be healthy, strong, smart, loving, and peaceful. You can know that God is the true Parent of everyone, including your brothers and sisters and even your parents. Knowing what's true about yourself and others is a prayer that heals.

Read a testimony related to this healing on page 249, "Claim Your True Inheritance."

LAZARUS BROUGHT BACK TO LIFE

When Jesus healed the man in Jerusalem who was blind from birth, ⊙ many scribes and Pharisees argued with him. They refused to believe that he healed through the power of God. Some even tried to kill him.

But Jesus and his disciples escaped from Jerusalem, which was in Judea, and crossed the Jordan River to Perea. The people there came and listened to him. Many believed that God sent him and

To find more information on color-coded terms, see pages 261–282.

CONCEPTS | CUSTOMS | GLOSSARY | PEOPLE | PLACES

SEE "Man Healed of Blindness from Birth," p. 134.

In John 11:2 the Bible tells us that Mary anointed Jesus' feet at a dinner where Jesus was the honored guest. This dinner occurred after Jesus had restored Lazarus to life. Mary spread precious perfume on Jesus' feet and wiped them with her hair, showing her deep love and gratitude for Jesus and her loyalty to him (see John 12:1–9). This is not the same woman who washed Jesus' feet at the home of Simon the Pharisee (see Luke 7:36–50; "Woman Healed of Sin," p. 50).

that his power to heal came from God.

Then, Jesus' good friends Mary, 💬 her sister Martha, and their brother Lazarus needed his help back in Judea. Lazarus had become very sick. The sisters were worried about him, so they sent a message to Jesus saying, "Lord, the friend you love is sick." The sisters didn't ask Jesus to come heal their brother, but they probably hoped he would.

When Jesus received the news about his friend Lazarus, he said, "This sickness is an opportunity to prove that death has no power. The Son of God is going to show people the wonderful goodness and power of God. And because of this, the Son will be respected and honored." Jesus was speaking of himself when he used the term "Son of God."

The Gospel of John describes Jesus' conversation with his disciples this way: "Jesus answered, Are there not twelve hours in the day? If any man walk in the day, he stumbleth not, because he seeth the light of this world. But if a man walk in the night, he stumbleth, because there is no light in him" (John 11:9–10).

The Jewish concept of a day included twelve hours for day and twelve for night. Jesus encouraged his disciples to learn as much as they could from him during the time he had left with them—comparing this time to the daylight. He compared night to the time when he would be gone and couldn't teach them any longer.

Jesus loved Martha and her sister and Lazarus, but he didn't leave right away to help them. That might seem surprising, but Jesus was praying about what to do. He knew that God, who is good, creates everyone and never takes life away. He knew Lazarus was safe in God's love—forever. Jesus was listening for God's thoughts, or angel messages. He knew God would tell him just the right time to go to Bethany, the village in Judea where Lazarus and his sisters lived.

After two days, Jesus knew it was time to go. He said to his disciples, "Let's go back to Judea."

The disciples did not want to go. They said, "Master, the Jewish leaders tried to kill you the last time you were there. Why do you want to go back?"

Jesus reminded his disciples that he was the **light of the world**. This light was the truth about God's all-power and goodness that Jesus trusted completely. His mission was to bring this light of truth to the world. Since this mission was God-directed, it could not fail, and he had to complete it. Going to Judea and healing Lazarus was part of that mission. He wanted his disciples to see that they were part of his mission, too. They needed to be by his side to learn from him. There would be a time soon when he would not be with them, so he wanted them to learn all they could now.

Next, Jesus said to them, "Our friend Lazarus is asleep. I'm going to wake him up."

His disciples didn't understand. They said, "Lord, if he's asleep, he'll be all right."

But Jesus didn't mean that Lazarus was sleeping. This time he explained, "Lazarus is dead. And for your sakes, I'm glad I wasn't with him because now you'll really learn to trust God." He knew that what they would see would help them understand that God is the only power. Jesus said strongly, "Let's go to him now."

Even without hearing anything more from Mary and Martha, Jesus knew that Lazarus had died.

Jesus had brought people back to life at least twice before. (See "Widow's Son Brought Back to Life," p. 45; "Jairus' Daughter Brought Back to Life," p. 69). But restoring those two people to life happened so quickly after they had died that some may have wondered if the people were really dead. This time there would be no doubt.

Being buried for four days had special meaning to the Jews. They believed that people had a spirit that waited by the grave for three days, hoping to return to the body. But on the fourth day, when the body began to decay, the spirit left forever. Raising the dead would have been surprising after even a day or two, but the passage of four days made this resurrection to life astonishing.

Thomas, one of the twelve disciples, said to the others, "Let's go to Judea and die with Jesus." Thomas thought he and the other disciples might be killed there, but he was brave and loyal to Jesus. His bravery must have helped the other disciples because they all decided to go. They left Perea with Jesus and headed to Bethany.

As they came near the village, Jesus learned that his friend Lazarus had been buried four days earlier.

Bethany was about two miles from Jerusalem. Many Jews had come from Jerusalem to be with the sisters while they mourned for their brother.

The minute Martha found out that Jesus was just outside of Bethany, she hurried to meet him. But Mary stayed at the house, sitting quietly with those who had come to visit her.

Martha's first words to Jesus were, "Lord, if you had been here, my brother wouldn't have died. But I know that even now, God will give you whatever you ask."

Jesus said, "Your brother will come back to life again."

Martha believed that Lazarus would come back to life—but not right then. She said, "I know my brother will come back to life in the resurrection on the 'last day.'" "Resurrection" means "rising from the dead." Many Jews believed that they would rise from death on a special day they called the "last day."

But Jesus wanted Martha to understand that he had the power to bring her brother back to life right then. He said to her, "I am the resurrection and the life." Jesus then told Martha that if someone who had died believed in his power over death, the person would rise again and understand that life never ends. And if someone living believed in his power over death, he or she would not die. He asked Martha, "Do you believe this?"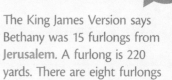

The King James Version says Bethany was 15 furlongs from Jerusalem. A furlong is 220 yards. There are eight furlongs in a mile, so 15 furlongs is just under two miles.

SEE **Jewish Customs— Mourning**, p. 268.

SEE **Faith**, p. 263.

Martha's statement that Jesus was the Christ showed her deep spiritual understanding and set forth an important point in Christianity. It was such an important point that when Peter later made a similar statement, Jesus said that God had revealed this truth to Peter. Jesus then established his church on that truth—the divine nature of the Christ (see Matthew 16:16–18).

The Bible says Jesus "groaned" (John 11:33). The Greek words here can mean he was "disturbed," "distressed," or "indignant." Here are some reasons Jesus may have been disturbed:

- His friends' limited faith and their disbelief in his mission
- The lack of faith among so many of the Jews
- The depth of Mary's grief

Martha answered him, "Yes, Lord, I do believe that you are the **Christ**, the Son of God, the one the prophets promised would come into the world." Martha may not have understood everything Jesus said, but she did believe he was the Christ, sent by God. With this new hope that her brother might be brought back to life, she hurried off to get her sister Mary.

Martha called Mary away from the people who were with her and whispered, "The Master is close by and wants to see you."

Mary jumped up and rushed to Jesus. The others thought she was running to the tomb to cry about her brother's death, so they hurried after her. As a result, Mary didn't have much time to talk with Jesus alone. When she saw him, she fell down in front of him. Then she said the same thing her sister had said: "Lord, if you had been here, my brother wouldn't have died."

But Jesus didn't answer her. Mary and the others were crying loudly. Jesus probably wished those he loved and taught, like Mary, had a more spiritual view of life. He wanted them to have **faith** that Lazarus could come back from the dead. It must have been hard for Jesus when he saw that they still didn't fully trust God's power, so he sighed. Then Jesus said, "Where did you put him?"

The people answered, "Come and see."

PROVERBS 12:28

"In the way of righteousness is life; and in the pathway thereof there is no death."

Jesus walked in the "way of righteousness." He prayed constantly—filling his thought with good ideas from God. He knew what was right and true—that God, Spirit, creates us. That means our life is really spiritual and perfect. This life never ends in death. It is forever. Jesus proved that knowing what is right and true is powerful—it can heal people and restore them to life. We can know what is right and true, too—just as Jesus did. Then we will be able to feel the same power of divine Life that brings healing and resurrection.

Tears came to Jesus' eyes, and he followed the people to the tomb. Some of them thought he was crying because his friend had died. They said, "Look how much he loved him." Others were not so kind. They said, "If he healed the man born blind, why couldn't he keep his good friend from dying?"

Again, Jesus let out a deep sigh. He knew that no matter what anyone said, death had no power because God, divine Life, is the only power.

When Jesus got to the tomb, he stopped. A round stone covered the opening. He gave this order: "Take away the stone."

SEE Jewish Customs—Burial, p. 267.

Some men rolled the big, heavy stone along the groove in front of the tomb so that it no longer covered the opening.

Earlier, Martha had told Jesus that she had faith in him. But now she was afraid again and thought he had come too late. She warned him, "He's been in there four days."

Jesus reminded her, "Didn't I tell you how important it is to trust God? Didn't I tell you that you'd see God's wonderful goodness and power?"

The crowd probably stepped back as the men rolled the huge stone away.

But Jesus stayed put. He looked up and away from the tomb and said, "Father, thank you for hearing my prayer." Jesus listened to God day and night and had complete faith in his Father-Mother God. He knew God was always loving him and guiding him. Every healing was an answer to prayer.

Jesus wanted the people to know he had prayed. So he said to his Father-Mother God, "I know that You always hear me. But I'm speaking aloud to You so that the people standing here will believe that You sent me."

Then, with a loud voice, Jesus shouted, "Lazarus, come out!" Jesus knew Lazarus needed to wake up from believing he had died. He needed to see that God gave him life that would never end.

Lazarus probably moved slowly because his arms and legs had cloth strips around them that had once been wet with spices and oil but were now dry and stiff. And since his head was wrapped in a cloth, he couldn't see.

What can YOU do?

Sometimes people are sick or sad for so long that it seems like their problem can't be healed. If that ever happens to you, and people say it's too late for you to be healed, don't believe them. Even though others had given up on trying to help Lazarus, Jesus didn't give up. He knew Lazarus was created by God and that God kept him safe forever. God's love and care never end. Jesus' great faith and understanding of God's power and love raised Lazarus from death. You can know that God, who made you and cares for you every day and every night, is always telling you the truth about your life. As you listen for God's good thoughts, you'll be healed, too. It's never too late for God!

The people watched the entrance to the tomb. They were amazed when Lazarus appeared. His body was still wrapped in cloth strips, and his head was wrapped in another cloth. Jesus said to the crowd, "Loose him and let him go."

Jesus had told his disciples he was going to wake Lazarus up from sleep. And that's just what he did. In fact, he woke up everyone that day—just as if they were having a bad dream. They had been dreaming that sickness and death had power, but Jesus knew what is really true—that God, good, is the only power. He proved that God loves everyone and keeps us all safe from sickness and death. He proved that life is eternal—it never ends.

What a wonderful day for Lazarus, Mary, Martha, and everyone!

BARTIMAEUS HEALED OF BLINDNESS

You can find other accounts of this healing in Matthew 20:29–34 and Luke 18:35–43.

After Jesus brought his friend Lazarus back to life, many Jewish leaders were jealous and began planning how they could get rid of Jesus.

Jesus left the Jerusalem area and went with his disciples to stay in a small town several miles away. When it was almost time for the **Feast of Passover**, Jesus decided to travel back to Jerusalem. On the way, he and his disciples passed through the city of Jericho. A large

The Jewish leaders (see Scribes, p. 277 and Pharisees, p. 275) were actually planning to arrest Jesus and then kill him. To read about Jesus restoring Lazarus to life, see "Lazarus Brought Back to Life," p. 140.

To find more information on color-coded terms, see pages 261–282.

CONCEPTS | CUSTOMS | GLOSSARY | PEOPLE | PLACES

Different Gospels tell this healing in different ways. Mark says Bartimaeus was the son ("bar" means "son") of Timaeus (see Mark 10:46). Matthew says there were two blind men but doesn't give their names (see Matthew 20:30). Luke says there was one unnamed blind man (see Luke 18:35).

group of people crowded around Jesus. Some were following him, and others lined up along the road to try to see him.

A blind man named Bartimaeus sat by the road begging. Earlier, he must have learned about Jesus and his healings and believed Jesus could help him.

Jesus was a common name, so using Jesus' hometown—calling him "Jesus of Nazareth"—helped distinguish him from others named "Jesus."

When he heard people in the crowd saying that Jesus of Nazareth was right there, Bartimaeus began to shout, "Jesus, Son of David, have mercy on me." The name "Son of David" meant "Messiah" or "Christ," a name the Jews used for a special king or prophet they believed would come one day to help and heal them.

The crowd told Bartimaeus to be quiet. But he wouldn't give up. In fact, he shouted even louder, "Son of David, have mercy on me."

Even with all the noise of the crowd, Jesus heard Bartimaeus and stopped. He said, "Tell that man to come here." Wherever Jesus was, he cared about people. He saw them as God saw them—as God's perfect, spiritual image and likeness. Seeing people this way healed them.

Now, instead of trying to quiet the man, the crowd said to him, "Cheer up. He's calling you." Throwing aside his cloak, Bartimaeus jumped up and went to Jesus. He must have known he would be healed.

Jesus asked him, "What do you want me to do for you?"

Bartimaeus answered, "Teacher, I want to see." Earlier Bartimaeus had called Jesus a name meaning "Messiah," which showed that he believed Jesus had power from God to help him. Now, he called him "Teacher," one who taught the law of God.

Here are some possible reasons the people told Bartimaeus to be quiet:

- They were trying to listen to Jesus teach as they walked.
- They didn't want Jesus to be bothered by beggars.
- Jesus' friends didn't want people to hear Jesus being called "Son of David." This meant "Messiah" and might attract the attention of the Jewish leaders, who were looking for Jesus to have him arrested.

A cloak is a long, loose piece of clothing, usually with short sleeves, that was worn over a coat. These might be reasons Bartimaeus threw his cloak aside:

- He wanted to get to Jesus quickly, and the cloak might slow him down.
- As a beggar, he may have used his cloak for collecting alms (money). By taking off his cloak, he might have been showing that he was sure he would be healed and wouldn't need his beggar's cloak anymore.

Luke tells us that Jesus said, "Receive thy sight" (Luke 18:42).

Matthew says that Jesus had compassion on two blind men. He touched their eyes, and they were healed (see Matthew 20:34). (See **Healing by Touch**, p. 267.)

I CORINTHIANS 2:5

"Your faith should not stand in the wisdom of men, but in the power of God."

Jesus had complete faith that the power of God is the only power in the world. He proved God's power again and again. We, too, can have faith that stands with God and God's power. We can be confident that God loves us and is able and ready to meet all our needs. Right now, we can prove how powerful God is to heal and help us—just as Jesus proved it two thousand years ago.

Jesus said to him, "Go on your way."  Jesus was telling him he already had his sight. Then he said to him, "Your **faith** has healed you." Jesus wanted Bartimaeus to know that he was healed through his trust in the power of God. Instantly, Bartimaeus understood—and he could see.

Bartimaeus was filled with joy. He could see with his eyes. And he could see—understand—with his heart the power of God's

Read a testimony related to this healing on page 247, "Vision Restored after Eye Injury."

law of good. Now, he wanted to be a disciple. So he joined right in with those following Jesus up to Jerusalem.  Everyone must have been really happy that day! ■

When Bartimaeus "followed Jesus," it probably meant that he became a disciple (Mark 10:52). Jesus had many more disciples than the twelve described most often in the Bible.

What can YOU do?

If you ever have a sickness that seems hard to heal, it may be discouraging. But think about Bartimaeus. When he learned that Jesus was nearby, he knew he could be healed. You, too, can know that you can be healed. Nothing is too hard to heal because nothing is impossible to God. And even though Jesus isn't here anymore, God is always with you. You're God's image and likeness. Since God is perfect, you are perfect, too. And since God loves you always, God keeps you perfect. Let God's truth be the only thing you know. Never give up on the truth. You can be healed.

LUKE 19:1–10

ZACCHAEUS HEALED OF DISHONESTY

On his way to Jerusalem for the **Feast of Passover**, Jesus passed through the city of Jericho, where he healed Bartimaeus of blindness.  As Jesus was traveling, people crowded around him to see and hear him. In the crowd was a man named Zacchaeus. He was the chief publican, or tax collector, in the area. His job was to collect tax money for the Romans. Zacchaeus was rich, and like most tax

SEE "Bartimaeus Healed of Blindness," p. 151.

Zacchaeus was a Jew. The name "Zacchaeus" means "pure," "righteous," "innocent."

SEE Roman Empire, p. 281.

To find more information on color-coded terms, see pages 261–282.

CONCEPTS CUSTOMS GLOSSARY PEOPLE PLACES

Here are two other reasons Jews didn't like Zacchaeus:

- He worked for the Romans, who were Gentiles. Therefore, he was considered "unclean" (see **Laws of Cleanness**, p. 268).

- Because he worked for the Romans, he was considered a traitor to his fellow Jews.

This was a strange thing for a very important tax collector to do. People would probably have laughed at him, but Zacchaeus didn't care. He really wanted to see Jesus—and up in the tree, he could do that. Although the Bible calls this a "sycamore" tree (Luke 19:4), it wasn't like sycamore trees today. We would call it a mulberry fig tree. These trees have low, wide-spreading branches that make them easy to climb.

collectors of that time, he had probably gotten rich by being dishonest. Often, tax collectors charged higher taxes than the Romans asked for and then kept the extra money. Because of this, the Jews didn't like Zacchaeus.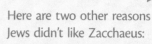

Zacchaeus must have heard about Jesus and how he loved everybody—even tax collectors and sinners (people who did wrong things). He wanted to see Jesus, but Zacchaeus was so short that he couldn't see over the crowd. Then Zacchaeus got a bright idea!

He ran ahead and climbed up into a tree so that he would be able to see Jesus when he passed by. When Jesus got close to the tree, he looked up into the branches and saw Zacchaeus. Although Jesus was not from Jericho, he probably knew who

What can YOU do?

Do you know someone who has done bad things to you or to others? There is something you can do about it. You can listen to God! God's angel thoughts will remind you that you are created by God—everyone's true Father and Mother. God loves everyone. And no matter what they have done, the way God knows them is what's true about them. God's children are spiritual, created in God's image and likeness—pure and perfect. God always sees them that way and keeps them that way. When you see people as God sees them, you'll begin to find the good in them. And both you and they will feel the healing power of God's goodness.

The Roman law said that a thief must pay back four times as much as was stolen. But the Jewish law only required that a thief pay back what he had taken plus one-fifth more (see Leviticus 6:1–6). Zacchaeus promised to pay back more than was required by the Jewish law—this showed how sorry he was.

Zacchaeus was and what people thought of him. But Jesus also knew that God, who is Spirit, created everyone in God's image and likeness. Jesus didn't think of Zacchaeus as a greedy, dishonest tax collector. He saw him as God's spiritual child—perfect and good.

Jesus called out to him, "Zacchaeus, hurry! Come down! Today I must be a guest at your house." Zacchaeus must have been very surprised. He scrambled down the tree as fast as he could and happily welcomed Jesus into his house.

But not everyone was happy about what Jesus had done. The crowd began to grumble. They didn't understand why Jesus, a great teacher, had gone to the house of a sinner—someone who was "unclean," or "impure." But that's not how Jesus thought of Zacchaeus.

Jesus saw Zacchaeus as good and pure, not as greedy and dishonest. This helped Zacchaeus see himself that way too. Zacchaeus stood up straight and made a promise. He said, "At this moment, Lord, I'm going to give half my money to poor people. And if I have cheated anyone, I will pay back that person four times more than what I took."

Jesus said to him, "Today, healing has come to this family, for this man is also a son of Abraham." Jesus may have meant that Zacchaeus was healed of his sin because he was like Abraham—

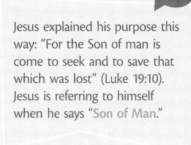

Jesus explained his purpose this way: "For the Son of man is come to seek and to save that which was lost" (Luke 19:10). Jesus is referring to himself when he says "Son of Man."

who had **faith** in the one God. What he said may have helped people change their view of Zacchaeus and his family and start to see them as "clean," or "pure."

Jesus said, "My purpose in life is to look for and to heal those who have lost their way." Jesus loved and cared for everyone, even those who had let bad thoughts and actions make them forget God's goodness.

Zacchaeus must have been so glad to be free of the bad thoughts and behavior that had probably made it hard for him to feel close to God, who is all good. And what a great lesson everyone else learned that day—to see sinners as God's children, loved and cared for by their Father-Mother God. ■

I THESSALONIANS 5:15

"See that none render evil for evil unto any man; but ever follow that which is good, both among yourselves, and to all men."

Jesus knew that even if someone has done bad things, just as Zacchaeus had, it's never helpful to be mean to the person. When Jesus met Zacchaeus, he didn't think of him as a sinner who had done bad things. He saw the man God had created, who is good and pure and could never do anything wrong. When people we see or know are doing bad things, we can do as Jesus did. We can pray. Our prayer can be to see them as God's spiritual, perfect children. And just as this clear view healed Zacchaeus of sin, our prayers can heal sin today.

Read a testimony related to this healing on page 245, "Honesty Is the Only Policy."

159

LUKE 22:47–51

MALCHUS' EAR HEALED

After healing people in Jericho, Jesus continued to Jerusalem. Within a short time, he and the disciples arrived for the **Feast of Passover**. During Passover week, Jesus told his disciples that he would be crucified. This would be their last Passover meal together. During this meal, Jesus said that one of them would betray

SEE these stories about Jesus' healings in Jericho:

- "Bartimaeus Healed of Blindness," p. 151

- "Zacchaeus Healed of Dishonesty," p. 156

Jesus would be arrested, turned over to the Romans (see Roman Empire, p. 281), and punished by crucifixion (being nailed to a cross and left there to die).

To find more information on color-coded terms, see pages 261–282.

| CONCEPTS | CUSTOMS | GLOSSARY | PEOPLE | PLACES |

him. He meant that one of the disciples would turn him over to the Jewish leaders who wanted to arrest him and have him killed.

After the meal, he left the city with eleven of the disciples to go to the **Mount of Olives**. There, among the olive trees in a place called Gethsemane, Jesus asked his disciples to pray. He then went a little distance away to pray by himself. When he returned to the disciples, they were asleep.

During the Feast of Passover, Jews prepare a special meal to celebrate the escape of the Jewish people from slavery in Egypt. The Passover meal Jesus ate with his disciples before his crucifixion has since been called the "Last Supper."

Matthew and Mark give the name of this garden, Gethsemane, which is across the eastern valley from Jerusalem on the Mount of Olives. Jesus often went there to pray. It was an olive orchard, and there was a press to squeeze oil from the olives. "Gethsemane" means "oil press."

As Jesus was praying, he hoped God would save him from being crucified. But most important of all, he wanted to obey God. That's why Jesus prayed, "Not my will, but thine, be done" (Luke 22:42).

161

Matthew and Mark say that Jesus asked some of his disciples to pray with him more than once. But each time, after going off to pray alone, Jesus came back and found them sleeping. (See Matthew 26:36–43; Mark 14:32–41.)

The Gospels tell us who the people were who came to arrest Jesus: chief **priests**, elders, **scribes**, captains of the **Temple**, men and officers sent by the chief priests, and **Pharisees**. Both Jews and Romans were part of the group. The Gospels also say that these men came with swords and clubs, lanterns and torches. (See Matthew 26:47; Mark 14:43; Luke 22:52; John 18:3.)

John says that when Jesus saw Judas and the group of men coming closer, he stepped forward to meet them and asked them who they were looking for. They replied, "Jesus of Nazareth." He then told them, "I am he." The Greek words here are actually "I am," without the word "he." **CONTINUED**

162

Jesus told them it was important for them to pray. While he was speaking, they heard people coming up the hill toward them.

As the people came closer, Jesus and the disciples could see that it was a large group. And leading them was Judas, one of Jesus' twelve disciples.

Judas walked right up to Jesus and was ready to kiss him on the cheek. This is how friends said "hello" to each other in that country. But Jesus stopped Judas with these words: "Are you going to point me out to the enemy with a kiss?"

This must have been very hard for Jesus and the eleven loyal disciples! Judas had been their friend, traveling with them, learning from Jesus, and even being sent out with them to heal. And now Judas had betrayed Jesus and was bringing soldiers to arrest him.

The frightened disciples asked Jesus, "Lord, shall we fight them with our swords?"

Suddenly, Peter took out a sword and struck Malchus, a servant of the high priest, or head priest, at the Temple. Peter cut off Malchus' ear. Instantly Jesus said, "Enough of this. Let them have their way." He was telling the disciples that this was not the right way to fight back. Jesus met hatred with love. He did not let anger and fear control him.

Then, with soldiers all around ready to arrest him, Jesus reached out with love and touched

CONTINUED

"I Am" is a name for God. By saying God's name, Jesus may have been stating that God's power was present right there where they were and that there was no other power. The men felt the power of Jesus' answer. They immediately fell on the ground (see John 18:4–6). Jesus knew that the soldiers were powerless to do anything to him unless he allowed it.

According to Matthew and Mark, Judas actually kissed Jesus, saying "Hail, master," or "Master, master" (Matthew 26:49; Mark 14:45).

These are some of the reasons Judas may have betrayed Jesus:

- He was greedy for money. He sold Jesus' location to the Jewish leaders for 30 pieces of silver.
- He wanted to be popular and was jealous of Jesus' goodness and power.
- His jealousy made him ungrateful for all the good Jesus had done.

Only John tells us the names of the disciple, Peter, and the servant, Malchus (see John 18:10).

What can YOU do?

Sometimes someone may act like an enemy and try to hurt you—by hitting you or hurting your feelings or trying to get you in trouble. And you may think the best thing to do is to hurt back. But Jesus showed his disciples—and us—a much better way to respond. When enemies came to arrest Jesus and harm him, he was ready with powerful thoughts of love. Instead of getting angry, Jesus stayed calm. Instead of hating, Jesus showed love. Instead of hurting back, Jesus healed. As we listen to God's messages, we'll find ways to be calm, show love, and heal, too.

 SEE Healing by Touch, p. 267.

Read a testimony related to this healing on page 260, "Football Injury Healed."

Malchus' ear. It was healed right then! Jesus prayed all the time, so he was ready and willing to help and heal anyone, anywhere, anytime—even if it was an enemy like Malchus. He knew the truth about all people—that they were God's children, spiritual and perfect.

Right in the middle of hatred and fear, Jesus showed the healing power of God's love. What a lesson for everyone! ∎

LUKE 22:42

"Not my will, but thine, be done."

Jesus knew that God is Love and is the only power in the universe. Therefore, God's will, or plan, always blesses everyone. When something in his life was hard to face, Jesus prayed to let go of what *he* thought should happen and to trust *God's* plan. When something in our life seems hard, we can trust God, too. We'll find that everyone involved is blessed when we do that. Each day we can turn to God with the same prayer Jesus prayed in Gethsemane: "Not my will, but thine, be done."

JOHN 20:1–29

JESUS' RESURRECTION

You can find other accounts of this healing in Matthew 28:1–10, 16–20, Mark 16:1–18, and Luke 24:1–12, 36–49.

Jesus had been crucified. 💬 Joseph of Arimathea, 💬 who was secretly a disciple of Jesus, asked Pilate, the Roman governor, to let him take Jesus' body and bury it. 🔍 Pilate said he could do that.

💬 This man was a member of the Sanhedrin, the council of Jewish leaders in Jerusalem.

💬 The Jewish leaders turned Jesus over to the Romans, falsely accusing him of stirring up the people and wanting to be king. Pilate, the Roman governor, didn't think Jesus had done anything wrong. But the Jewish leaders insisted that he had and that he should be killed. After a while, Pilate gave in to their demands and ordered Jesus to be crucified—nailed to a cross and left there to die. (See Matthew 27:1–2, 22–26; Mark 15:1, 12–15; Luke 23:4, 13–14, 20–24; John 18:27–28; John 19:4, 14–16.)

To find more information on color-coded terms, see pages 261–282.

| CONCEPTS | CUSTOMS | GLOSSARY | PEOPLE | PLACES |

🔍 **SEE** Jewish Customs—Burial, p. 267.

This man was a synagogue ruler, a teacher of the Jews, and also a member of the Sanhedrin. Once, he met with Jesus in secret—during the night—to talk with him (see John 3:1–13).

A tomb is often referred to as a "sepulchre" in the Bible.

SEE **Sabbath Laws**, p. 269.

This woman was from Magdala, a city on the Sea of **Galilee**. She was a faithful **disciple** of Jesus. The Bible says Jesus healed her of seven devils. The number of devils indicates that her illness was very great (see Mark 16:9; Luke 8:2). She should not be confused with the sinful woman Jesus healed (see "Woman Healed of Sin," p. 50). Mary was probably wealthy because the Bible says that she and many other women used their own money to help Jesus (see Luke 8:3). Mary was at Jesus' crucifixion and was the first person Jesus appeared to after he rose from the dead (which is referred to as his "resurrection").

Another secret disciple named Nicodemus came with expensive spices. He helped Joseph prepare the body for burial. The two wrapped it in linen cloths and used the spices to perfume it. After this, the two men placed the body in an empty tomb. The tomb was carved out of a cave that was in a garden. A heavy, round stone was rolled in front of the entrance to the tomb to close it.

Jesus was crucified on a Friday. The two men had to prepare his body for burial very quickly because the Sabbath began at sundown. Jewish law did not allow any work to be done on Saturday, which was the Sabbath.

On Sunday morning, while it was still dark, Mary Magdalene went to the tomb. She was a friend and disciple of Jesus.

When she got to the tomb, she was shocked—the heavy stone had been rolled away from

Matthew, Mark, and Luke mention the other women who went with Mary Magdalene to the tomb. They include Mary, the mother of James; Salome, the mother of two of the disciples—James and John; Joanna, the wife of Herod Antipas' steward—who was in charge of Herod's house and all his servants; and other unnamed women. Mark and Luke say that the women were bringing spices to perfume Jesus' body some more. Because Joseph and Nicodemus had prepared the body very quickly, the women wanted to complete the preparation (see Matthew 28:1; Mark 16:1; Luke 24:1, 10).

The book of John says the two were Peter and the disciple "whom Jesus loved" (John 20:2). No one knows for sure who this disciple is. Many people think it was John, who was probably the youngest of the twelve disciples. He was known for his love for others as well as Jesus' love for him.

the entrance! Mary thought someone had taken Jesus' body.

She ran quickly and found Peter and another of Jesus' disciples. She told them, "They took the Lord from the tomb,

While John doesn't mention the other women, Mary's remark to the two disciples makes it clear that other women were with her when she went to the tomb. Luke says that Joanna and "Mary the mother of James" were among the other women (Luke 24:10).

The Jewish leaders had asked Pilate to seal the tomb and put guards there to watch it for three days in case Jesus' disciples came to steal the body and then say that Jesus had risen from the dead. Information from this time suggests that several Roman soldiers may have been at the tomb (see Matthew 27:63–66).

Joseph of Arimathea and Nicodemus used a lot of spices (75 pounds) to prepare Jesus' body for burial. In Jesus' time, spices—myrrh and aloes—were mixed with olive oil to make a paste or ointment. This ointment was then applied to the linen cloths that were wrapped around the body.

and we ••• don't know where they have put him!" •••

Right away, the two ran as fast as they could to see if what Mary had told them was true.

The other disciple got to the tomb before Peter. He stooped

down at the entrance and saw the linen cloths that had been wrapped around Jesus. But he didn't go into the tomb.

Peter was right behind him. He went right in and saw the linen cloths, too, but Jesus' body was not there.

Then the other disciple went into the tomb as well. This time, when he looked at the burial cloths, he knew right away that Jesus had risen from the dead.

The two disciples didn't stay at the tomb. Instead, they went back to their house.

John says that Peter and the other disciple didn't think about the **Old Testament** Bible verses that, hundreds of years earlier, told about Jesus' crucifixion and resurrection. But the other disciple still knew that Jesus had risen from the dead (see John 20:9).

Here are possible reasons why these two disciples left the tomb so quickly:

- They may have been afraid that, if the authorities (either Roman or Jewish) found them there, they would think they had stolen the body.
- They may not have known exactly what to do, since they didn't know where Jesus might be.
- They may have wanted to be someplace safe while they thought about Jesus' resurrection and what they would do next.

Matthew, Mark, and Luke each present different details:

- A great earthquake and an angel rolling back the stone from the opening of the tomb
- The tomb guards shaking and then becoming frozen with fear when they see the angel
- A young man in a long, white garment and two men in shining garments

(See Matthew 28:2–4; Mark 16:5; Luke 24:4.)

But Mary, who had returned to the tomb, stayed there, sobbing and crying out with grief. She knelt down to look into the tomb and saw what appeared to be two angels in white clothing. Mary heard them say to her, "Woman, why are you crying?"

She replied, "Because my Lord has been taken away, and I don't know where they have put him."

Then, she turned and looked back. She saw someone standing there. It was Jesus—but Mary didn't recognize him. She thought it was the person who took care of the garden. Jesus said to her, "Woman, why are you crying? Who is it you're looking for?" •••

Mary said to him, "Sir, if you are the one who took him, tell me where you have put him, and I will come and get him."

Jesus spoke to her again. He said, "Mary!" When she heard him call her by name, she knew it was Jesus! She turned toward him and said to him, "Rabboni," meaning **Teacher.** •••

Mary may have reached out to cling to Jesus because he said to her, "Don't hold on to me." He must have sensed that she was trying to hold on to him as a person instead of holding on to the truths he had taught her. He told her, "I'm still ascending." ••• Jesus hadn't yet risen completely above material thinking and life—but his final **ascension** was coming soon. While he was still with Mary, he was encouraging her to think more spiritually. Instead of depending on him to help her, he wanted her to know she could depend on God.

Next, Jesus told her, "Go to the disciples—my brothers—and tell them I am ascending unto our Father, to our God." ••• Jesus loved the disciples and wanted them to know he thought of them as

To read about Jesus' treatment of women, see "Woman/Women," p. 278.

"Rabboni" is another word for "rabbi." Both are Hebrew words meaning "teacher."

The word "ascending" means "rising up" or "going from a lower to a higher level." In this case, it means that Jesus' thinking was becoming entirely spiritual.

Matthew says that Jesus told Mary not to be afraid. She was to tell the disciples that they should go to Galilee, where they would see him (see Matthew 28:10).

Mary was chosen to take this message to Jesus' disciples. That was a big job, but because of what Jesus had told her, she must have realized she could do it. Since she is the one who delivered this message to them, Mary is often called the "apostle to the apostles."

Mark and Luke say that, before Jesus visited the disciples in a group, he spoke with two disciples who were walking along the road. These two then went and told the larger group that they had seen Jesus (see Mark 16:12–13; Luke 24:13–35).

brothers. His Father, God, was also their Father. He wanted them to understand that their Father would be with them forever to help them.

Mary did exactly what Jesus asked her to do and went straight to the disciples. She told them she had seen Jesus and delivered his message to them. What an amazing day—their Teacher had risen from the dead!

That evening, Jesus went to see the disciples. They weren't sitting out in the open because they were afraid that the Jews who had been so angry at Jesus might try to hurt them. Instead, they were gathered in a room with the door closed.

When Jesus arrived, he didn't knock on the door and wait for someone to open it. He just appeared in the room. It may be that his thought was so spiritual at that point that nothing could stop him from being where he needed to be.

Luke says the disciples were frightened by Jesus' appearance because they thought he might be a spirit (see Luke 24:36–37).

Jesus knew that appearing suddenly like that might startle the disciples, so right away he told them, "Be at peace." But the disciples were still very surprised! They couldn't believe that Jesus was right there with them. Then he showed them the marks on his body from the crucifixion, and they knew for sure it was Jesus. They were so happy to have their Teacher with them again!

ROMANS 8:6

"For to be carnally minded is death; but to be spiritually minded is life and peace."

Jesus proved by healing and by raising people from the dead how powerful spiritual thinking and prayer are. One way Jesus prayed was by knowing with all his might that God, Spirit, is the only reality or power. He knew that being materially minded leads to sickness, sin, and death. But being spiritually minded—having faith in God, Spirit—leads to health and life. Jesus prayed by keeping his thought filled with love, goodness, purity, harmony, health, so he was always ready to help and heal others. Each day, he turned his thought away from the problems he saw with his eyes and accepted, instead, only spiritual perfection and the power of God. Spending his days knowing what was true about God and God's children prepared Jesus for his resurrection. And his resurrection helps us see that we, too, can rise above wrong thoughts—including thoughts of death—to know that the joy and peace and life God gives us never end.

SEE Matthew 12:38–42;
Matthew 16:21; Matthew 17:22–23;
Matthew 20:17–19; Mark 8:31;
Mark 10:32–34; Luke 9:22;
Luke 18:31–33.

SEE John 21:1–14.

What can YOU do?

People may say that being raised from death is impossible. But the Bible teaches us that nothing is impossible to God. Jesus proved this. He raised himself as well as at least three other people from death—the son of the widow from Nain, Jairus' daughter, and Lazarus. Jesus taught the importance of loving God with all your heart and mind and soul. That means not giving any power or place to anything unlike God.

Think of each day as an adventure in learning to see what is true about yourself and others as God's perfect, spiritual children instead of as material bodies. You can shut out any lies that say evil is real, fill your thinking with good, spiritual ideas from God, and hold on to them. As you do this, you'll be building your ability to destroy the belief that you—or anyone else—can be sick or sinful or can die. And you'll rise a little each day—making steady progress in your understanding that God, Spirit, is your life.

Jesus had told the disciples he would rise on the third day after his crucifixion, but they had not understood that this would really happen. Not until they saw Jesus standing in front of them did they realize what he meant.

Thomas wasn't with the disciples when Jesus met with them on the day of his resurrection. But eight days later, Jesus met with them again, and Thomas was there this time. Jesus also met with seven of the disciples one morning on the shore of the Sea of Tiberias.

These meetings with the disciples helped them understand that Jesus' teachings were true. With his spiritual understanding of God's power and love, their Teacher had overcome death and risen from the grave. Jesus' resurrection lifted the disciples' thoughts higher so they could see that death could be overcome and that life never ends. ■

JESUS' ASCENSION

You can find another account of Jesus' ascension in Mark 16:19–20.

Soon after Jesus' resurrection,  he saw a few of his disciples, who told the rest of the group that their **Master** had risen from the grave. But the ones who hadn't seen Jesus couldn't believe he was alive. That evening, when the disciples were gathered together, Jesus visited them. Then everyone there realized that Jesus had overcome death. This strengthened their **faith** in God as the only power.

SEE "Jesus' Resurrection," p. 165.

SEE Mark 16:9–13.

SEE Matthew 28:16–20; Mark 16:14–18; Luke 24:36–48; John 20:19–23.

To find more information on color-coded terms, see pages 261–282.

CONCEPTS CUSTOMS GLOSSARY PEOPLE PLACES

175

Jesus reminded his disciples of the power of their complete faith when he told them, "If you believe in the Christ, you can heal, and you will be safe." (See Mark 16:15–18.)

 SEE John 20:26–29; John 21:1–14.

 SEE Acts 1:3.

JOHN 12:32

"And I, if I be lifted up from the earth, will draw all men unto me."

When Jesus said these words, he wasn't talking about lifting up a human body above the ground. He was referring to the Christ and to our thoughts. Jesus lifted up the Christ by seeing people as God's children—perfect and spiritual—instead of getting dragged down into thinking of them as limited human beings. This spiritual view drew people to him. They were drawn to the God-given goodness Jesus saw in them. They knew that this view could help them, and it did—they were healed. As we lift up our thinking by seeing the Christ in others, we'll find people attracted to our spiritual view of them, too. And, like Jesus, we'll have opportunities to help and heal.

Jesus talked with his disciples for a while that night. He encouraged them to follow his example and to heal the same way he did—through complete faith in God's all-power and goodness. God's children are made perfect—and God keeps them that way. This perfect, spiritual selfhood, which belongs to everyone, is the **Christ**.

Jesus met with the disciples a few other times after his resurrection. He knew he would soon be leaving this group of men and women, and he wanted to keep teaching them for as long as he could.

Then, 40 days after his resurrection, Jesus led the disciples to Bethany. When they got there, he raised his hands and blessed them, and as he was blessing them, he **ascended**.

The word "ascend" means to rise up or go from

SEE Mark 16:19; Luke 24:51; Acts 1:9.

a lower to a higher level. And that's exactly what happened. Jesus rose above all thought of life as material. His understanding of God as Spirit and of life as spiritual was so complete at that point that the disciples, who were more material in their thinking, couldn't see him anymore. He had disappeared from their sight.

But he wasn't leaving them alone. They had the Christ to comfort and guide them. With the Christ—the understanding of their own and others' spiritual nature—they could continue following Jesus' example. And they did. After Jesus' ascension, the disciples went on to teach and to heal and even to bring people back to life.

The Christ is still with us today, showing us how to follow Jesus' example, too.

What can YOU do?

After the ascension, Jesus' disciples no longer had him right by their side to answer their questions or help them when a problem seemed too big to handle. But that didn't stop them from sharing Jesus' teachings or from healing. In fact, they became better healers and teachers because, instead of depending on Jesus, they had to rely on their own understanding of the Christ—the truth of everyone's nature as children of God. We can't talk to Jesus in person either, but we have the Christ with us, just as the disciples did.

You, too, can deepen your understanding of the Christ by seeing your own and others' Godlike qualities. You can know that God makes people kind, not mean. God makes them healthy, not sick—happy, not sad. This is true about each of us, even when it doesn't look that way. By seeing others as spiritual, not material—by seeing them the way God made them—you're taking your thought to a higher level. You're ascending out of material thinking. The disciples proved that seeing the Christ in others lifts thought to a spiritual level and heals. You can prove that, too!

Other New Testament HEALINGS

PETER AND JOHN HEAL MAN OF LAMENESS

Jesus was the greatest spiritual healer in the world.

He had many disciples, or students, but he chose twelve to be his closest disciples. Peter and John were part of that group. Jesus sent the twelve, and many others, to cities and towns to share the good news about God's love and power and to heal people. When the disciples went out, they were known as "apostles."

To find more information on
color-coded terms, see pages 261–282.

CONCEPTS | CUSTOMS | GLOSSARY | PEOPLE | PLACES

Jesus had promised his apostles that they would not be alone after he left them. He told them they would be filled with the **Holy Spirit**, which is also called the Holy Ghost.  This meant they would understand that God is Spirit and that God's children are always spiritual, perfect, healthy, and loving. With this powerful spiritual understanding, they could do what Jesus had asked them to do—go out into the world and heal people.

Not long after Jesus **ascended**, many of his followers, including the twelve apostles, were together in **Jerusalem** for the religious **festival** called **Pentecost**. Suddenly, they were filled with the Holy Spirit, and what Jesus had taught about God's great love became very clear to them all at once. When this happened, they told the large crowd at the festival about the power of God—and they told them in such a way that each one there could understand.

The **Jews** were expecting the Messiah, or **Christ**, to come someday to help and heal them. But Peter, standing with the other apostles, explained that Jesus was the Christ. He spoke of Jesus' wonderful healings and told about how he had risen from the dead. He also said that Jesus had been filled with the Holy Spirit. Peter explained that this same spiritual power and understanding had filled the apostles that very day and that everyone could receive this same power. That day, three thousand people believed Peter and became followers of Jesus!

After Judas betrayed Jesus, there were only eleven apostles. When Jesus **ascended**, the apostles prayed to know who should take Judas' place. They chose a man named Matthias who had been with them continually, even from the time Jesus was baptized by John (see Acts 1:21–26).

SEE Acts 1:8.

SEE Matthew 10:5–8.

SEE "Jesus' Ascension," p. 175.

SEE Acts 2:1–8.

SEE Acts 2:22–32, 36.

Peter also told the people to "repent, and be baptized" (Acts 2:38). One meaning of "repent" is to turn away from wrong thinking and turn toward God. Peter was telling the Jews that they could have a new life by following Jesus, whose teachings and healings showed that God is unlimited Love. (See also **Baptism**, p. 262.)

SEE Acts 2:38–41.

At one point after the Pentecost, Peter and John were walking to the **Temple**. It was three o'clock in the afternoon—one of the three times each day that Jews in Jerusalem went to the Temple to pray. A man was there who had never been able to walk. Every day people carried him to the Temple gate called "Beautiful" so that he could beg for money. When he saw Peter and John going into the Temple, he asked them to give him something.

Peter and John looked right into the man's eyes, and Peter said firmly, "Look at us." Peter wanted this man to pay attention to them.

The man obeyed Peter and looked up at them—expecting them to give him something.

Jesus had taught Peter and John well. He had shown them how important it is to see people the way God made them—happy, healthy, strong, and always the image and likeness of their Father-Mother God. So Peter and John thought about this man as the likeness, or reflection, of God and God's goodness.

Peter said to him, "I don't have money, but I will give you what I do have. In the name of Jesus Christ of Nazareth, rise up and walk." Peter wanted this man to know that he was being healed by the same understanding of God's power and goodness that allowed Jesus to heal.

In the Bible a name represents the nature or character of someone. When Jesus' followers said they were doing something in the "name of Jesus **Christ**," they meant that they had **faith** that the same healing power God gave Jesus was also given to them.

Jewish laws said that anyone who touched someone sick or disabled should not enter the **Temple**. But Peter didn't let that stop him from reaching out to this man and lifting him up. Peter knew that both he and the man were God's spiritual, perfect children, so they could never be unclean or imperfect.

JOHN 14:12

"He that believeth on me, the works that I do shall he do also; and greater works than these shall he do."

Jesus was a great teacher who showed his disciples how to heal and how to pray with complete faith in God's goodness and love. They learned to trust that God, who creates everyone spiritual and perfect, never gives anyone anything but good. We, too, can have faith that God always cares for us and the world. This leads to wonderful healings—just as it did for Jesus' disciples.

Then Peter took the man by the right hand and lifted him up. Right away, the man's feet and ankle bones were strong and firm. Peter's words and actions showed his **faith** that the man was God's spiritual, perfect child—and therefore he could walk. This faith helped the man trust that he could walk.

What can YOU do?

What if you're not feeling well and can't seem to do the things you usually do? Remember the lame man at the Temple gate who had never walked. When Peter told him to get up and walk, the man obeyed. Peter and John had learned from Jesus that everyone is made in the image and likeness of God, spiritual and perfect. They knew that if something was not spiritual and perfect, God hadn't made it, so it had no power. You can know that, too. Taking a stand for what is good and true will help you feel like your true self again.

Now that the man was healed and considered "clean," Jewish law allowed him to go into the Temple and be with his family and friends.

The man jumped up, stood, and started walking. For the first time in his life, he could enter the Temple! 💬 He was so happy as he went in with Peter and John that he was leaping and shouting out his thanks to God.

Everyone around them saw this man walking and jumping. They knew he was the beggar at the Beautiful Gate who had never walked. They were amazed and wondered how this had happened.

185

Read
a testimony related
to this healing
on page 253,
"Ankle Injury Healed."

Solomon's Porch was one of the covered walkways lined with marble columns that surrounded the Temple area. It was built by King Herod in the same area as the original porch built by King Solomon. Jesus taught there, and so did the apostles.

The man was so full of joy that he grabbed on to Peter and John and wouldn't let go. As the three reached the place in the Temple called Solomon's Porch, all the people there ran to see this wonderful healing that had happened.

Think what it meant to the man to be able to walk! And think what it meant to the people to see him healed. They must have been so happy to know that those who understood Jesus' teachings could heal just as Jesus had. ■

STEPHEN HEALS MANY PEOPLE

At one point when Jesus was still with his apostles, he told them that soon they would be filled with the **Holy Spirit**. That meant they would be filled with spiritual thoughts about God and God's power.

Just as Jesus had promised, the apostles received the Holy Spirit on the day of **Pentecost**. Right away, they were eager to share

 SEE Acts 1:8. The King James Version uses "Holy Ghost" for "Holy Spirit" here, but many translations use "Holy Spirit."

To find more information on color-coded terms, see pages 261–282.

CONCEPTS | CUSTOMS | GLOSSARY | PEOPLE | PLACES

What can YOU do?

Stephen showed that whatever God asks us to do is important. He was given a job—to help care for Jesus' followers—and did it gladly. But he didn't stop there. Understanding the power of God's love, Stephen also healed and shared the good news of Jesus' healings and teachings. You can listen for God's special ways to help others, too.

 **SEE** Acts 2:1–8.

See Acts 2:41. In some cases, the Bible uses the term "disciples" to refer to Jesus' followers (see Acts 6:1). In other cases, it uses the term "brethren," which means "brothers" or "brothers and sisters" (see Acts 6:3).

 **SEE** Acts 6:1–6.

their new understanding and to encourage others to have **faith** in the teachings of **Christ** Jesus.

As a result, more and more people became followers of Jesus. There were so many that the twelve apostles couldn't take care of everyone. So they asked the followers to choose seven men to help them. These men needed to be good and wise and filled with spiritual understanding and power. One of the men chosen was Stephen. But Stephen did more than help the apostles take care of the followers.

Stephen also healed. He had great faith in God and in Jesus' teachings. Stephen knew, as Jesus did, that everyone is created in the likeness of God—spiritual and perfect—and that God gives only good. Because of Stephen's great faith, he was able to heal many people.

The Bible calls Stephen's healings "wonders and miracles" (Acts 6:8).

Stephen was also a good speaker. He listened to God so that he would know just what to say to others. He helped many people learn more about God's power and goodness and about Jesus' life and healings. Because of this, even more people became followers of Jesus' teachings.

The early followers were happy and thankful to have this great healer and speaker with them! ▪

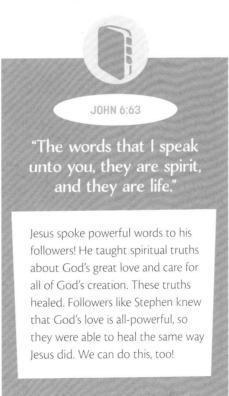

JOHN 6:63

"The words that I speak unto you, they are spirit, and they are life."

Jesus spoke powerful words to his followers! He taught spiritual truths about God's great love and care for all of God's creation. These truths healed. Followers like Stephen knew that God's love is all-powerful, so they were able to heal the same way Jesus did. We can do this, too!

Not everyone was happy about Stephen's healing work. Some of the Jews accused him of speaking against Moses, so Stephen defended himself before the Jewish council. He said that, in the past, Jewish leaders had resisted the idea that God is Spirit. As a result, they had worshiped God with material rituals in a material place—the Temple. Stephen explained that Jesus, the **Messiah**, had given them a more spiritual way to worship, but instead of following Jesus' teachings, they had crucified him. After Stephen spoke, the Jewish leaders were so angry that they killed Stephen (see Acts 6:9–15; Acts 7:1–60).

ACTS 8:5–8

PHILIP HEALS PEOPLE OF ILLNESSES, PARALYSIS, AND LAMENESS

SEE Acts 6:1–6. The King James Version uses "Holy Ghost," but many translations use "Holy Spirit."

SEE Acts 8:1–4.

Like Stephen, Philip was one of the seven men chosen to help the apostles take care of Jesus' many followers, especially the widows. These men were wise and filled with the Holy Spirit.

Soon after these men were chosen, the scribes and Pharisees in Jerusalem began to treat Jesus' followers very badly. Because of this, many of the followers, including Philip, left the city quickly.

Philip went to a city in Samaria and taught the people there. Most Jews didn't travel through this area because, for many years,

To find more information on color-coded terms, see pages 261–282.

CONCEPTS | CUSTOMS | GLOSSARY | PEOPLE | PLACES

the Jews and Samaritans had not been friends. They had argued
for a long time about the right way to worship God and about who
had the best place to worship God.

But these arguments hadn't stopped Jesus from loving the
Samaritans. Once while he was visiting a city in Samaria called
Sychar, he had a long conversation with a woman. He explained to
her that God is Spirit, so the best way to honor God is to worship
God spiritually—in thought. He said the place where you worshiped
didn't matter. Jesus also told her that he was the Messiah, or **Christ**.

What can YOU do?

Sometimes when people are mean to others, you may feel sad or upset. You might even be tempted to stop doing what's right. If that happens, remember Philip. When people were mean to Jesus' followers, he didn't give up on doing good. Philip listened to God's direction and went to new places where he could keep helping others. Like Philip, you can listen to what God is telling you to do. You can know that evil has no power to stop good because God is the only power. When you listen to God's thoughts, which are always good, you'll see that nothing can steal your happiness or stop you from doing good.

 SEE John 4:5–30, 39–42.

Philip's teaching and healing in Samaria reminded Jesus' followers that their mission was for the whole world and not just for the Jews.

She was so excited about what she had heard that she told many others. A lot of Samaritans came and listened to what Jesus said and believed that he was the Christ.

Jesus had also told his followers that, after he was gone, they should go to Samaria and to other places to teach everyone about the Christ. Philip was one of the first followers to go to Samaria.

The people who heard Philip teach paid attention to what he said because he healed many people who were sick, mentally ill, paralyzed, or lame.  Philip was filled with the Holy Spirit— with spiritual thoughts about God's love and power. He knew that everyone is created spiritual and perfect, in the image and likeness of God, who is Spirit. Philip was sure that God gives only good, and he was able to heal because of this **faith** in God's goodness and care.

The Samaritans were happy to have Philip with them. They were very grateful to see so many wonderful healings! ■

Read a testimony related to this healing on page 248, "Surrounded by Love at Camp."

Here, the King James Version refers to those with mental illnesses as having "**unclean spirits**" (Acts 8:7).

PROVERBS 3:5

"Trust in the Lord with all thine heart; and lean not unto thine own understanding."

Philip was filled with the spiritual understanding of God's goodness and power. He didn't let wrong thoughts crowd out his trust in God. We, too, have spiritual understanding right at hand to help us with whatever problem we may have. We can have faith that God created us perfect and keeps us that way. There is no power other than God, who is all-powerful. So there is no reason to be afraid. Trusting God with all our heart brings healing.

ACTS 9:1–19

ANANIAS HEALS SAUL OF BLINDNESS

You can find other accounts of this healing in Acts 22:3–16 and Acts 26:4–18.

Every day, more and more people were becoming followers of Christ Jesus. Saul, a Jew living in Jerusalem, was not happy about this, so he decided to do something about it. He started going to the followers' homes and dragging both men and women outside and taking them to prison. Many fled Jerusalem, hoping

 **SEE** Acts 8:3.

Here, the Bible calls Jesus' followers "any of this way" (Acts 9:2), probably because Jesus called himself "the way, the truth, and the life" (John 14:6).

Two other accounts say that it was noon when Saul and those traveling with him saw this light that was much brighter than the sun (see Acts 22:6; Acts 26:13).

To find more information on color-coded terms, see pages 261–282.

CONCEPTS CUSTOMS GLOSSARY PEOPLE PLACES

that Saul wouldn't find them.

Saul knew that many followers had escaped to Damascus, so he decided to go after them. He asked the high priest of the Sanhedrin for letters he could take to the synagogues in Damascus, where the followers were preaching about Jesus. These letters told the synagogue leaders that he had the right to bring Jesus' followers back to Jerusalem to put them in prison. 💬

But something happened when Saul was on his way to Damascus...

Suddenly a very bright light shined all around him. 💬 He called this a light from "heaven," which shows that he felt God was present with him. When he saw this light, he fell to the ground. Then he heard a voice saying to him, "Saul, Saul, why are you doing these terrible things to me?"

Saul shook with fear and was amazed. He replied, "Who are you, Lord?" 💬

Saul also asked, "Lord, what wilt thou have me to do?" (See Acts 9:6 in the King James Version. Many other translations include this in Acts 22:10.)

195

In Acts 9:5, the King James Version adds that Jesus told Saul, "It is hard for thee to kick against the pricks." (This sentence is also found in many other translations in Acts 26:14.) A "prick" was a sharpened stick that farmers used to guide farm animals in the right direction. Jesus was saying that just as a farm animal who resisted following a farmer's direction would feel pain from the prick, Saul was feeling pain from not obeying God's direction.

Another time when Saul, who was also known as Paul, told about this experience, he said that Jesus gave him special instructions about taking the message of Christ Jesus to others (see Acts 26:16–18).

Paul's other two accounts of this story give slightly different details (see Acts 22:9; Acts 26:13–14).

The voice said, "I am Jesus, and you are doing terrible things to me. Get up and go into the city. There, you will be told what you must do."

The men traveling with Saul stood still and didn't say a word. They had heard the voice, but they didn't see anyone talking.

When Saul got up, he couldn't see at all. The people with him had to lead him by the hand the rest of the way to Damascus.

He spent three days there not able to see. During that time, he didn't eat or drink.

A disciple of Jesus, a man named Ananias, lived in Damascus. Ananias was a faithful Jew who obeyed the Jewish laws. Other Jews liked and respected him.

Maybe Saul didn't eat or drink because he was upset and confused about what had happened. But he was also a faithful Jew, so he might have fasted (not eaten) because that was one of the ways Jews expressed devotion to God or showed sadness for doing wrong.

SEE Acts 22:12.

MATTHEW 5:43–44

"It hath been said, Thou shalt love thy neighbour, and hate thine enemy. But I say unto you, Love your enemies, bless them that curse you, do good to them that hate you, and pray for them which despitefully use you, and persecute you."

When someone hates us, it can be hard not to hate that person back. But Jesus said to love our enemies. He taught us to see those who hate us as God sees them—as God's lovable, pure, and perfect children. When our thoughts are like God's thoughts, good things happen in our lives.

197

Judas was a common name. This Judas is not the same person as the man who betrayed Jesus.

The Bible says that Saul had a vision of Ananias "putting his hand on him, that he might receive his sight" (Acts 9:12). Putting hands on someone symbolized the power of God to heal. (See **Healing by Touch**, p. 267.)

Ananias had a vision where Jesus spoke to him, saying, "Ananias!" He answered, "Yes, Lord, I am here." Then Ananias heard Jesus say, "Get up and go to Straight Street. Find Judas' house and ask for a man from Tarsus named Saul. At this very moment, Saul is praying. He has seen in a vision a man named Ananias coming into the house and healing him of his blindness."

But Ananias didn't really want to go to Saul. He answered, "Lord, many people have told me about this man and the terrible things he did to your followers in Jerusalem. Now, he's here in Damascus—and he has permission from the chief priests to make your followers prisoners and take them back to Jerusalem to be punished!"

But Jesus in the vision said to Ananias, "Go to Saul. I have chosen him to take my message to the Gentiles and to kings, as well as to the Jews. I will explain to Saul that taking the good news to others will not be easy." Jesus knew that not everyone would understand or accept this spiritual message. Saul would have to be strong in his **faith** in God because at times people would be very mean to him.

Ananias listened and obeyed. He went to the house where Saul was staying. After going in, he touched Saul and said to him, "Brother Saul, Jesus, who spoke to you in a vision as you were coming here, talked with me, too. He sent me to you so that you could see again and be filled with the **Holy Spirit**." Immediately, Saul was able to see, and he got up. He had a new understanding of God's goodness and power, and he was healed.

Ananias knew that nothing is impossible to God, so he trusted Jesus' message that Saul would become one of his followers. Jesus had proved the power of God by healing. He had given his followers

The Bible says that Jesus called Saul a "chosen vessel" (Acts 9:15). In Greek the word "vessel" can mean anything that is useful or helpful. Saul would go on to teach people about Jesus and heal people just as Jesus had. Saul also brought Jesus' message to the Jews, who the Bible calls the "children of Israel" (Acts 9:15). They were given this name because they were descendants, or "children," of the twelve sons of Jacob, who was also called "Israel." Jacob was one of the Jews' most honored ancestors.

By using the term "brother," Ananias was welcoming Saul into the family, or fellowship, of Jesus' followers.

The Bible says that it was as if "scales," or flakes, had fallen from Saul's eyes (Acts 9:18).

If people are really mean to you, it may be hard to forgive them. But you can remember Ananias and how he forgave Saul. You can know, as Ananias did, that God, who is Love, cares for everyone. Even if someone acts in a mean way, that person is really God's child—perfect and loving. Bad actions are like a mask or costume that someone has put on—they aren't ever part of anyone's real self. The spirit of love that God gives you wipes away hurt or hate. It frees you to be kind and to share the love that's always in your heart.

an understanding of God's love for everyone. Ananias knew how important it was to forgive Saul—because expressing God's love brings healing.

Next, Saul was baptized. Sometimes people were baptized by being washed in water. This showed that they had become Jesus' followers. **Baptism** was also a way for people to show that they had gotten rid of wrong thoughts and were now listening to God.

Saul felt the power of the Holy Spirit—the Spirit of truth.

He had not eaten for three days, but now he was ready to have a meal. Ananias and Judas, the owner of the house, and some other followers may have eaten with Saul as a way of showing that they forgave him and trusted him. Their forgiveness would have made Saul's faith in Jesus' teachings even stronger. After this, Saul stayed with Jesus' followers in Damascus for several days.

What an amazing journey Saul wound up having! He had gone to Damascus to do terrible things to Jesus' followers, but, instead, he was healed by one of them. Not only could he see with his eyes, but he could also see, or understand, the truth about Jesus. Saul became one of Jesus' most faithful followers and learned to teach and heal the way Jesus did. ◼

PETER HEALS AENEAS OF PARALYSIS

On the day of Pentecost, Jesus' apostles and other followers were filled with the **Holy Spirit**. They knew that God is Spirit, the only power, and that God is always present to heal. After that, the apostles healed many people in Jerusalem through the power of God. 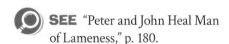 And large crowds of both men and women became followers. After Peter healed a man who had never walked, 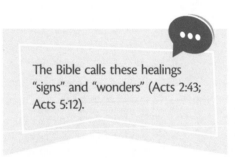 people

The Bible calls these healings "signs" and "wonders" (Acts 2:43; Acts 5:12).

SEE "Peter and John Heal Man of Lameness," p. 180.

To find more information on color-coded terms, see pages 261–282.

CONCEPTS | CUSTOMS | GLOSSARY | PEOPLE | PLACES

ISAIAH 40:29

"He giveth power to the faint; and to them that have no might he increaseth strength."

Peter knew that God, who is Love, is powerful and tenderly cares for everyone. Peter also knew that Love would strengthen and heal Aeneas. And he was right! We, too, can feel divine Love right here and now, caring for and strengthening us—and everyone.

brought the sick into the streets on their beds so that if Peter passed by, he would heal them. Many from outside Jerusalem also brought those who were sick—and they were all healed!

SEE Acts 5:12–16.

SEE Acts 9:31.

All over Palestine, Jesus' followers began meeting in groups, which they called "churches." The followers had a deep love for Jesus and his teachings. They were filled with spiritual understanding and the power of God—and this comforted and encouraged them. New people kept joining the churches.

What can YOU do?

You may know someone who has a disability—maybe he or she can't walk very well or can't hear or speak clearly. Like Peter, you can fill your thoughts with God's tender love for that person. Your good thoughts are a prayer that can help bring healing.

Peter traveled around the country visiting these groups and talking with the followers. He brought the good news about Jesus and what he had taught of God's powerful love and goodness.

One of the towns Peter visited was Lydda. There, he found a man named Aeneas, who was paralyzed. For eight years, Aeneas had stayed on his bed because he couldn't walk. When Peter saw Aeneas, he knew that he could help him. Peter had learned about healing from listening to Jesus teach and from watching him heal.

He had seen Jesus heal a man who was paralyzed. ⊙ And Peter himself had healed a man in Jerusalem who had never walked. ⊙

Peter spoke to Aeneas with great **faith** and strength. He said, "Aeneas, Jesus **Christ** heals you!" Peter was telling Aeneas that the healing power is the Christ, the spiritual nature of God that Jesus expressed. Jesus knew that everyone is made by God, in the likeness of God, who is Spirit. This likeness is spiritual and perfect, healthy and strong. Peter knew that this Christ-like thinking was his own thinking, too—and that it would heal Aeneas.

Next, Peter commanded him, "Get up and make your bed!" Peter was humbly trusting God's love for this man. He wanted Aeneas to see that he was completely well and didn't need to stay in bed. Instantly, Aeneas stood up. He was healed!

When the people who lived in Lydda and the area around it saw Aeneas walking, they became followers of Jesus' teachings! ■

⊙ SEE "Man Healed of Paralysis," p. 26.

⊙ SEE "Peter and John Heal Man of Lameness," p. 180.

The King James Version calls this area "Saron," which refers to the "Plain of Sharon"—the large area between Joppa and Caesarea. Many translations use "Sharon."

ACTS 9:36–42

PETER RESTORES TABITHA TO LIFE

Some **followers of** Christ Jesus lived in the city of Joppa, which was by the Mediterranean Sea. One of them, named Tabitha, loved people and did many good and kind things for those who needed help.

To find more information on color-coded terms, see pages 261–282.

CONCEPTS | CUSTOMS | GLOSSARY | PEOPLE | PLACES

But Tabitha became sick and died. The followers probably thought about Jesus, who had overcome death. Jesus knew that God, divine Life, is more powerful than death and gives life to everyone. And he proved this when he rose from the dead.

Knowing that Jesus had proved God's power over death must have strengthened the followers' trust in God and given them hope that their friend would come back to life. They were probably praying with all their might when they heard some wonderful news.

The followers learned that Peter was in Lydda, just a half-day trip away. They believed that Peter, who had great faith in God, could bring Tabitha back to life, so they sent two men to get him. When the men found Peter, they asked him to hurry back to Joppa. He went with them right away.

What can YOU do?

What can you do when you need help? You can do what the followers in Joppa did when their friend Tabitha died. They prayed, trusting God to give them the help they needed—and they got it. They learned that Peter was nearby. Peter had a great understanding of God's power to heal, so they sent for him to come and pray for Tabitha—and she was healed. When you need help, you can trust God, too. God's love and care are always with you to comfort you and guide you to the help you need.

 SEE "Jesus' Resurrection," p. 165.

207

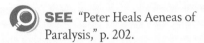 **SEE** "Peter and John Heal Man of Lameness," p. 180. And see Acts 5:12–16 to read about Peter healing many people in the streets of Jerusalem.

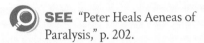 **SEE** "Peter Heals Aeneas of Paralysis," p. 202.

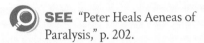 **SEE** these examples of Jesus restoring people to life:

- "Widow's Son Brought Back to Life," p. 45

- "Jairus' Daughter Brought Back to Life," p. 69

- "Lazarus Brought Back to Life," p. 140

Sometimes people built a room on the roof that could be used for various activities. They might visit with guests there or hold feasts or pray. The breezes made it a cool place to sleep in the summer.

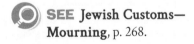 **SEE Jewish Customs— Mourning**, p. 268.

 **SEE** Matthew 9:23–25; Mark 5:39–40; Luke 8:51–54.

Peter had healed many in Jerusalem—a man at the Temple who couldn't walk, and other sick people who were brought to him. 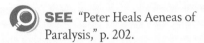 And people in Lydda were talking about another man Peter had healed—a man right in their own city who had been paralyzed.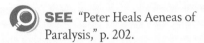

Peter had also seen Jesus bring several people back to life. 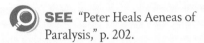 And Jesus' own resurrection from death showed Peter even more clearly that death could be overcome. Peter had learned from Jesus' example that God, divine Life, is more powerful than death, and he was ready to prove God's great power.

When Peter came to the house, the followers took him to the upstairs room where they had laid Tabitha's body on a bed. Many women whose husbands had died were there. They were called "widows." Tabitha had helped them a lot, and they were very sad about her death. They may also have been worried about what they would do without her. When Peter arrived, they went over and stood beside him, crying loudly and showing him the clothes Tabitha had made.

Peter must have remembered something Jesus had done when he brought a young girl back to life. People had been crying loudly then, too 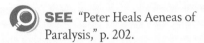—and Jesus had told them all to leave. 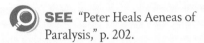 He didn't want people to be there unless they had faith in the power of God to bring someone back to life. So Peter did what Jesus had done—he sent all the crying women out of the room. Then he was alone with powerful thoughts of God's love for Tabitha. Peter was knowing with all his heart that divine Life—not death—is the only power.

Peter kneeled down to pray. He turned his thought away from death and listened only to God. The power to bring Tabitha back to life came from God—not from Peter. He must have felt the great power of God's love right there and knew it was stronger than death.

"When thou prayest, enter into thy closet, and when thou hast shut thy door, pray to thy Father which is in secret; and thy Father which seeth in secret shall reward thee openly."

Peter had learned from Jesus how to pray. He knew he needed to shut out all thoughts that were not about life and goodness. He needed to let his thinking be filled with messages from God. Peter knew that God, who is Love, fills all space and was holding Tabitha in the safety of God's love. Peter listened quietly, and God answered his prayer, as God always does, with happiness, peace, and healing. We can pray as Peter prayed and trust as Peter trusted. Then, we will hear God's answers to our prayers, too.

Read
a testimony related to this healing on page 255, "Victory over Death."

Peter then turned to the woman and said, "Tabitha, get up." And she opened her eyes. When she saw Peter, she sat up. Then, he took her by the hand and helped her get up from her bed. It was a very special moment—Peter had proved that divine Life has power over death.

Peter called the followers and widows who were waiting downstairs. He showed them that Tabitha was alive and well. Think what this meant to everyone! It strengthened their faith in God's power and God's care for all. News of this healing spread all over the city of Joppa. As a result, many more people believed in the power of God to heal and became followers of Jesus. ■

ACTS 14:1–3

BARNABAS—A HEALER WITH PAUL

You can find another account of Barnabas' healing work in Acts 15:12.

Barnabas **had great** faith in God. He was filled with the Holy Spirit—the truth that God is always present and all-powerful. Barnabas was a gentle man, and others liked him very much. Once he was kind to a man named Saul when other followers of Christ Jesus

To find more information on color-coded terms, see pages 261–282.

CONCEPTS | CUSTOMS | GLOSSARY | PEOPLE | PLACES

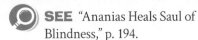

 **SEE** "Ananias Heals Saul of Blindness," p. 194.

SEE Acts 9:26–28.

As a Jew and a Roman citizen, Paul had both a Hebrew name (Saul) and a Roman name (Paul). See Acts 13:9.

JOSHUA 1:9

"Be strong and of a good courage; be not afraid, neither be thou dismayed: for the Lord thy God is with thee whithersoever thou goest."

If others are unkind to us, we don't have to be afraid—because God, who is Love, is always with us. Barnabas and Paul didn't let fear stop them from sharing God's truth, even though people were saying terrible things about them. They were so filled with the goodness and power of God that they stayed calm and just kept praying and teaching and healing. God helped them do what they needed to do, and God will help us, too!

were afraid of him because earlier Saul had tried to hurt the followers. Barnabas told them that Saul had changed and that he was now a follower of Jesus, too. He showed them that they could trust Saul.

A few years after this, Barnabas traveled with Saul, who was also called by his Roman name Paul. They went to many places to teach, to heal, and to start churches.

On their travels, Barnabas and Paul visited the city of Iconium. There, they spoke with great power and joy to both Jews and Gentiles about Jesus and his teachings. Many of these people became Jesus' followers. But some of the Jews were upset with Barnabas and Paul because they didn't like what they taught. These Jews turned some of the Gentiles against the two men as well.

But Barnabas and Paul kept preaching to the people. They stayed in Iconium for a long time and spoke boldly and without fear. Barnabas, like Paul, was very spiritually minded. He knew that everyone is created in the likeness of God, who is Spirit, and that God would never let that likeness be sick or in pain or disabled in any way. His thoughts were so filled with the Holy Spirit that there was no place for sickness in his thinking. Together, Barnabas and Paul healed many people in Iconium, and many of those who saw these healings were grateful to learn about God's love and to see that this love heals. ■

What can YOU do?

Have you ever seen others treat someone unkindly and wanted to help but not known if you should? Maybe you were afraid that if you helped, your friends might make fun of you. If that happens again, you can let God's love fill your heart. God is our Father-Mother, tenderly caring for everyone. You can know that God blesses you and helps you be kind and loving. No matter what anyone says, your good thoughts and prayers will help both you and others. God's great love is with everyone—forever.

PAUL HEALS MAN OF LAMENESS

Just before his experience at Damascus, Saul tried to get rid of the followers of **Christ** Jesus. But after his wonderful healing, he was changed forever, and he became a follower, too. ◉ During the next few years, Saul spent time in several different areas. Sometimes he was being quiet, thinking and praying and learning about Jesus' life and teachings. Sometimes he was talking to others about Jesus. At one point, a follower named Barnabas went to Saul's hometown of Tarsus to find him and bring him back to Antioch. Then Barnabas and Saul, who was also called Paul, traveled together to many cities, including Iconium, teaching, healing, and starting churches. 💬

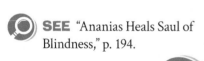

◉ **SEE** "Ananias Heals Saul of Blindness," p. 194.

💬

John Mark, another follower, joined Saul and Barnabas on the first part of their trip (see Acts 12:25).

To find more information on color-coded terms, see pages 261–282.

CONCEPTS | CUSTOMS | GLOSSARY | PEOPLE | PLACES

Even though Paul and Barnabas healed many people in Iconium, some of the people there turned the crowds against them. ◉ Despite this, the men kept teaching and preaching in Iconium for a long time, but then they learned that there were plans to kill them. So they escaped to the city of Lystra and other places nearby, but they didn't stop preaching. 💬 They were so filled with the **Holy Spirit**—with spiritual power—that they told everyone who would listen about Jesus.

 SEE "Barnabas—A Healer with Paul," p. 211.

See Acts 14:1–7. After his healing of blindness (see "Ananias Heals Saul of Blindness," p. 194) and before the healing of the lame man described here, Paul visited these regions: Syria, Arabia, **Palestine**, Cilicia, Cyprus, Pamphylia, Pisidia, Lycaonia (see Acts 9:19–30; Galatians 1:15–17; Acts 11:22–30; Acts 12:24–14:3). In most of these places, he taught and healed, but the Bible doesn't have a record of all of those individual healings.

At the end of this trip, though, while in **Jerusalem**, Paul told the apostles about all the Gentiles he and Barnabas had healed through the power of God while they were traveling (see Acts 15:12). Healing was a natural result of Paul and Barnabas' **faith** in God's power and love for all, so it's not surprising that, wherever they went, people learned of their healing power, asked for help, and were healed.

In the crowd at Lystra was a man who really needed their help. He had never been able to walk.

Most of the people in Lystra were Gentiles—they didn't believe in the one God, who is Spirit. But this man was listening closely to what Paul had to say, and Paul could tell that he believed he could be healed.

 SEE Faith, p. 263.

215

What can YOU do?

If you ever have a problem that seems so big that you wonder if you have the faith to heal it, think about Paul. Even when he saw a man who had never walked, Paul was sure of God's power to heal. That's what faith is all about—trusting God. You can have strong faith, too. When you trust that the Almighty God makes the entire creation spiritual and perfect—and keeps it that way—you'll find your faith is powerful. The problem won't seem so big anymore. In fact, when you understand that God is in control, you'll find you're healed.

When Paul looked at the man, he didn't pay attention to what was wrong with him. Instead, he knew that God is Spirit and that this man was actually God's child—perfect and spiritual. He knew with all his heart that God had made this man perfect and was keeping him that way. Then Paul looked right at the man and said firmly, "Stand up!"

And he did! In fact, he jumped up and started walking. Paul's complete **faith** in God's goodness and love for God's children had healed him.

The man must have been so happy—and grateful—to walk for the first time in his life!

I CORINTHIANS 2:5

"Your faith should not stand in the wisdom of men, but in the power of God."

Paul was a great spiritual healer. He had strong faith—not in his own power to heal but in the power Christ Jesus had shown, which is God's power. Even when a problem seemed hopeless—like not being able to walk—Paul fully trusted God's power. He knew, as Jesus knew, that everyone is created in the image and likeness of God—spiritual and perfect—and God protects us from harm of any kind. We can know this, too, and heal just as Paul did. Our faith will then be "in the power of God."

Read a testimony related to this healing on page 255, "Grateful to God."

217

PAUL IS HEALED OF INJURIES

Paul **was in** Lystra, where he had healed a man who had never been able to walk. The people were amazed by this healing, but they didn't understand it. They believed in many gods, rather than the one God, and thought that Paul and his friend Barnabas, who was with him, were gods. So, they began to worship them. Right away, Paul told the people that there was only one God, who

SEE "Paul Heals Man of Lameness," p. 214.

The people of Lystra thought Paul and Barnabas were two of the gods they believed in. They thought Paul was Mercury (Hermes), the messenger of the gods, and Barnabas was Jupiter (Zeus), the king of the gods. They even brought oxen (with wreaths around their necks) to sacrifice to Paul and Barnabas (see Acts 14:11–18).

To find more information on color-coded terms, see pages 261–282.

CONCEPTS | CUSTOMS | GLOSSARY | PEOPLE | PLACES

created everything. He talked about God's goodness and explained that God gives good to everyone.

The people finally stopped trying to worship Paul and Barnabas, which was good—but then a bad thing happened. The same Jews who had turned the crowds against them in other cities came to Lystra. They got the people there so upset with Paul that they wanted to kill him, so they began throwing heavy stones at him. When they were sure he was dead, they dragged his body outside the town and left it there.

Paul must have been praying while he was being stoned. He was probably knowing that God was always taking care of him and that God's love would keep him safe. As he lay on the ground outside the town, some of Jesus' followers from Lystra gathered around him. They showed great love and bravery by coming to be with him. The followers had been learning from Paul about Jesus, who had overcome death, so they were probably praying that Paul would be healed, too.

Paul's teaching and healing convinced many Jews to become followers of Jesus. This often made the scribes and Pharisees jealous because they were losing their power and authority over the people.

The Bible does not say that Paul was dead but that those who stoned him "thought" he was dead, or were "supposing he had been dead" (Acts 14:19). Stoning was a harsh way to kill someone. Heavy rocks were thrown at the victim, usually until the person was dead. Paul was so badly injured that he appeared to be dead.

What can YOU do?

If it scares you to see others fighting or hurting each other, remember Paul when a crowd of people stoned him. When he saw those men coming toward him, do you think Paul knew that God was right there with him and that God's goodness was more powerful than stones? Yes! Paul was sure that nothing could separate him from God's love. His prayer helped him be brave and strong. Like Paul, you can know that nothing can ever separate you—or anyone—from God's care. When you fill your thought with God's love and power, you'll be less afraid, and you'll feel more certain that God keeps everyone safe!

Read a testimony related to this healing on page 244, "Healing Following a Fall."

Just then, Paul got up! And he walked right back into Lystra without fear. What an amazing healing! Paul had been so badly hurt that people thought he was dead, but now he got up and walked. His prayers, and those of Jesus' followers, were more powerful than the stones people had thrown at him.

ROMANS 8:16

"The Spirit itself beareth witness with our spirit, that we are the children of God."

God, who is Spirit, creates us, gives us energy, and keeps us alive. We are God's children, made in the likeness of Spirit—entirely spiritual. Nothing that happens to our human body can touch our real, spiritual life. Paul understood these truths. When angry men attacked him, he knew that nothing could take away his life. This understanding quickly healed his injuries and helped him get back to doing God's work. We, too, can know that our life and energy come from God, who is Spirit. Spirit keeps us safe forever.

What a wonderful proof of God's power! The followers must have been very happy and thankful that Paul was safe and well.

The next day Paul and Barnabas left for the city of Derbe—at least a day's trip on foot or by donkey. There, they continued teaching the good news about Jesus. And many more people became followers of Jesus' teachings! ■

ACTS 16:16-18

PAUL HEALS YOUNG GIRL OF MENTAL ILLNESS

A while after Paul was healed of his injuries from stoning,  he and Barnabas went to Jerusalem, where they told the followers there about the churches that were growing and the Gentiles who had been healed on their trip. Next, they went home to Antioch. Then, Paul and his new helper, Silas, began a new trip.

SEE "Paul Is Healed of Injuries," p. 218.

Paul visited many regions, including **Palestine**, **Phoenicia**, Syria, Cilicia, Lycaonia, Galatia, Pisidia, Mysia, Pamphylia, and Phrygia (see Acts 14:21–16:15). Later, Paul wrote to the Christian churches in Galatia, strengthening their **faith**. He reminded them that the healings happening among them were done through the **Holy Spirit** (see Galatians 3:5). Everywhere Paul traveled, he taught people about the power of Spirit to help and to heal.

To find more information on color-coded terms, see pages 261–282.

CONCEPTS · CUSTOMS · GLOSSARY · PEOPLE · PLACES

Two other followers joined Paul and Silas—Timothy at Lystra and Luke at Troas.

SEE Jews, p. 273.

What can YOU do?

What if someone keeps others from listening to your good ideas? Or what if you see people using someone else to make themselves richer or more powerful? You can know that everyone is controlled by God, who is good and is the only power. God makes everyone loving and good. You can see people the way God makes them and know that nothing can keep them from acting that way. God is always showing all of us who we truly are and what is best to do. God will show you how to stand up for what is right and help others.

First, they went back to many of the cities Paul had visited before, teaching the followers more about **Christ** Jesus and encouraging them.

Next, they set out to new cities, crossing the Aegean Sea to Macedonia. In the city of Philippi, they found a small group of Jewish women who met to pray together by a river. A woman named Lydia was with them. She loved Paul's teachings and became a follower of Jesus.

One day in Philippi, when Paul and his friends were on

🔍 **SEE** Demons, p. 263.

💬

The Bible says the girl was "possessed with a spirit of divination" (Acts 16:16). In Greek, the word "divination" is "Python." Python is also the name of a snake in a Greek myth. Many people believed this mythical snake controlled a priestess at the temple in Delphi, Greece. The people believed this snake was killed by a Greek god named Apollo, whose spirit then controlled the priestess. She acted strangely and muttered, and people believed she could tell what would happen in the future.

their way to the river to pray and worship God, a young girl met them. This girl had a mental illness. She acted strangely, sometimes speaking nonsense and shouting. The people believed she was controlled by an evil spirit. 🔍 They even thought this was a good thing because they believed she could tell them what was going to happen in the future. 💬 This girl was kept as a slave by men who collected money from people wanting her to tell them about their future. 💬

💬

Here, the Bible says this girl was "soothsaying," which means "telling the future" (see Acts 16:16).

The term "most high God" was used by both Gentiles and Jews:

• Gentiles used the term for Zeus—the greatest of the many Greek gods they worshiped. So when the girl used this name to describe Paul's God, it's possible people thought he believed in Zeus. Paul would not have wanted people to think this. He was teaching about the power of the one God, who is all good.

• Jews used this term for the one God. So people might have thought Paul was preaching about the Jewish faith. In a Roman city like Philippi, the idea that Paul was trying to convert Romans to the Jewish faith would have upset the Roman leaders (see **Roman Empire**, p. 281).

For many days, this girl followed Paul and his friends wherever they went, screaming, "These men are the servants of the most high God! They show us how we can be saved!" Her yelling made it hard for people to listen to Paul's teaching.

Paul wanted to be able to teach, and he cared about this young girl. He was also troubled because people believed evil spirits were

real and had power over her. He knew there is only one Spirit, God, who is always in control and gives only good. Paul also knew that by understanding this, Jesus had healed people with mental illnesses.

Paul turned toward the girl and said to the false evil spirits, "I command you in the name of Jesus Christ to come out of her." Paul knew that evil spirits weren't real—that they were only wrong thoughts. Paul was casting out, or getting rid of, these wrong thoughts through the same power of God that allowed Jesus to heal. Jesus had said, "You shall know the truth and the truth will make you free." And that's exactly what Paul did. He knew what was true about the girl as God's child, and she was healed.

Right away the girl was free and able to act normally. Paul had proved that God is the only Spirit. The girl must have been so thankful—and eager to learn more about Jesus and how he healed. ■

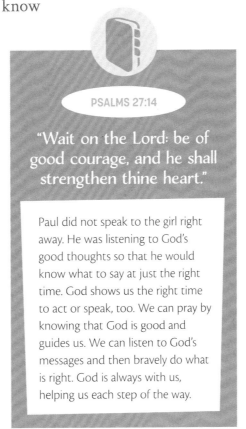

PSALMS 27:14

"Wait on the Lord: be of good courage, and he shall strengthen thine heart."

Paul did not speak to the girl right away. He was listening to God's good thoughts so that he would know what to say at just the right time. God shows us the right time to act or speak, too. We can pray by knowing that God is good and guides us. We can listen to God's messages and then bravely do what is right. God is always with us, helping us each step of the way.

In the Bible a name represents the nature or character of someone. When Jesus' followers said they were doing something in the "name of Jesus **Christ**," they meant that they had **faith** that the same healing power God gave Jesus was also given to them.

This was a brave action to take. The men who were keeping the girl as a slave would no longer be able to make money from her and would be very angry with Paul.

 **SEE** John 8:32.

PAUL RESTORES EUTYCHUS TO LIFE

Paul **had healed** a young girl in Philippi. 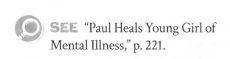 From there, he left to take his healing message to people in other cities and regions. Sometimes other followers of Jesus traveled with him. 💬

SEE "Paul Heals Young Girl of Mental Illness," p. 221.

Among the followers who traveled with Paul at different periods during this time were Silas, Luke, Timothy, and Aristarchus.

To find more information on color-coded terms, see pages 261–282.

CONCEPTS | CUSTOMS | GLOSSARY | PEOPLE | PLACES

From Macedonia, Paul sailed across the Aegean Sea to Troas, on the coast of Asia. Paul taught and healed in many regions: **Palestine**, Syria, Galatia, Phrygia, Asia, Macedonia, Illyricum, and Achaia (Greece) (see Acts 17:1–20:6; Romans 15:18–19).

The **Jews** considered Sunday the first day of the week. This day had special meaning for Jesus' followers because it was the day that his resurrection had taken place. The followers met on Sundays to eat and worship together. These gatherings were held in the evening because Sunday was a workday for them.

Once a week the early followers of Jesus came together to share a simple meal. Anyone could come—rich or poor, master or enslaved. Those who could brought food and in this way helped feed the followers who were poor.

CONTINUED ON NEXT PAGE

On one of his trips, Paul went to Greece and Macedonia and then sailed to the city of Troas. On the first day of the week, Jesus' followers gathered to pray and have a meal together. Often, they met in an upstairs room of a house.

CONTINUED FROM PREVIOUS PAGE

The main purpose of the meal was not eating but being together to pray and learn more about Jesus' teachings. Bread was broken, or torn into pieces, and passed around to be used for dipping into the food. After the meal, another prayer was shared. Sometimes the followers sang hymns or someone preached. Because these gatherings were loving and joyous, they have been called "love feasts" or "feasts of charity" or *agape*—the Greek word for "love." These feasts helped the followers feel they were a family. And it reminded them of the last meal the **disciples** ate with Jesus before he was crucified (see Matthew 26:26–28; Mark 14:22–24; I Corinthians 11:23–26). (See also **Church**, p. 270.)

Paul had been in Troas all week, but he was leaving the next day. So the followers were eager to hear him talk once more about **Christ** Jesus—his life, his teachings, and his healings. Paul spent as much time as he could with them—talking late into the night.

A young man named Eutychus was sitting on a windowsill listening to Paul. Many oil lamps were lit, and the room was probably very warm. Because of this and the late hour—it was around midnight—Eutychus fell sound asleep. Suddenly, he tumbled out of the third-story window to the ground. People rushed down the stairs to help him. When they picked him up, they found he was dead.

Paul went down to Eutychus, too. He bent over him, and, holding him in his arms, said to the others, "Don't be worried or sad. His life is in him." Paul refused to accept that Eutychus had died. He had **faith** in God's love and care for Eutychus and knew that God is the only power. Paul trusted God so completely that he left Eutychus and went back upstairs with the followers. He knew that God, divine Life, is more powerful than death, even though death seemed so real to the other people there.

Upstairs, Paul ate with the followers and talked with them for a very long time. He probably helped them understand why he had said Eutychus was alive when they believed he was dead. Paul may have talked to them about having faith in God's power. Perhaps he told them how Jesus had brought himself and others back to life. He probably discussed his own healings, too, including the time men threw stones at him and left him for dead. He had been healed of his injuries through God's power. Paul certainly had

 SEE these examples of Jesus restoring other people to life:

- "Widow's Son Brought Back to Life," p. 45

- "Jairus' Daughter Brought Back to Life," p. 69

- "Lazarus Brought Back to Life," p. 140

See "Jesus' Resurrection," p. 165, to read about Jesus bringing himself back to life.

 SEE "Paul Is Healed of Injuries," p. 218.

What can YOU do?

Those who were listening to Paul thought Eutychus was dead. But Paul refused to believe this. He knew in his heart what God knew—that Eutychus was God's spiritual child, full of life and energy. You can take steps every day to see more and more of God's all-power. You can reject thoughts of anything that is not like God and accept only what is good. By taking a stand for life, happiness, health, and safety, you will grow in your spiritual understanding and in your ability to prove God's presence in your life.

ROMANS 8:6

"To be carnally minded is death; but to be spiritually minded is life and peace."

Paul was very spiritually minded—filled with the understanding and power of God. So it was natural for him to understand that Eutychus was God's spiritual child, rather than to focus on his material body. When Eutychus died, Paul didn't accept that he was dead. His thought was filled with all the goodness of God—and he understood that God gives life that never ends. This spiritual-mindedness was powerful—it brought Eutychus back to life. Every day, we can learn more about God, who is Spirit, and depend on God to help and heal us. As we learn and grow spiritually, we'll understand more and more that God is definitely more powerful than death.

many wonderful proofs of the **Holy Spirit**—the understanding of God's all-power—helping and healing him.

When the sun came up, Paul left to continue his trip. The followers went to Eutychus and found him healed. They were so glad to see that he was alive. What a wonderful example of God's great power! Paul had showed them what Jesus had proved in his resurrection—that Life is more powerful than death. And they had seen it with their own eyes! ■

Read a testimony related to this healing on page 258, "When Our Son Was Hurt, We Turned to God."

PAUL HEALS HIMSELF OF SNAKEBITE

While in Troas, Paul brought a boy named Eutychus back to life.  After this, he went to Jerusalem. While he was there, some Jews from Asia said he had done something wrong. They made other Jews angry with him and even tried to kill him.

The Romans arrested Paul for starting trouble and began a long journey, taking him to appear before the authorities in Rome.

SEE "Paul Restores Eutychus to Life," p. 226.

SEE Roman Empire, p. 281.

To find more information on color-coded terms, see pages 261–282.

| CONCEPTS | CUSTOMS | GLOSSARY | PEOPLE | PLACES |

Luke and Aristarchus, two of Paul's friends, went with him. Along the way, the ship they were in stopped at Phoenicia and Lycia.

It was a hard trip because the sea was stormy and wild. High waves hit the ship and blew it off course. Even with all these difficulties, Paul was filled with the **Holy Spirit**—the great power and understanding of God. He took time apart from the others to pray.

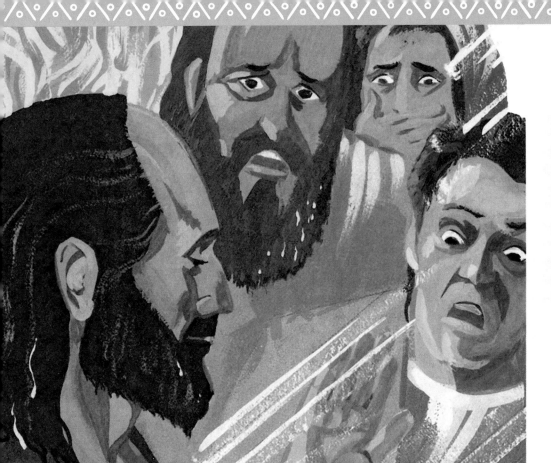

Here, the King James Version refers to these people as "barbarous." This doesn't mean they were wild or uncivilized. The Greek term means "foreigners." Other translations use the word "natives."

After several days of stormy weather, Paul gave everyone a comforting message from God. He told them that no one would be harmed—and no one was! Fourteen days into the storm, the boat crashed against rocks near an island, but everyone made it safely to shore.

When Paul and the others got to land, they discovered that the island was called Melita. The people who lived there were very kind. It was rainy and cold, and they welcomed Paul and the others by making a fire to warm them.

233

What can YOU do?

Have you ever felt afraid during a very bad storm? The storm Paul experienced was so bad that the ship he was in was wrecked. But Paul was so sure of God's love and care that fear couldn't find any place in his thoughts. His calm, clear thinking was a prayer that kept him—and his shipmates—safe. Paul knew that God can help no matter how scary a situation is. You can know this, too. God's goodness is with you now and always. You can feel safe wherever you are—even in a big storm—when your thoughts are filled with God's all-power and love.

Here, the Bible says "vengeance" would not let him live. The Greek word for "vengeance" is the name of the goddess of justice, Dike. These people believed that this Greek goddess would not allow Paul to live.

Paul helped keep the fire going by gathering a bundle of sticks. As he was laying the sticks on the fire, a poisonous snake slithered out, bit his hand, and held on tightly. When the people who lived on the island saw the snake hanging from Paul's hand, they said to each other, "Even though this man escaped from the shipwreck, he must be a murderer, and he won't be allowed to live." They believed that when bad things happened to people, it meant they had done something wrong and were being punished by one of their gods.

Paul didn't believe that, and he wasn't afraid of the snake. He knew that God is good and all-powerful and was always taking care of him. Therefore, nothing—not even that snake—had any power to hurt him. He just shook the snake off into the fire and wasn't at all hurt.

Those who lived on the island watched to see if Paul would swell up or fall down and die from the snakebite. When they saw that nothing bad happened to him, they decided he wasn't a murderer after all. Instead, they thought he must be a god. They did not understand how Paul's healing happened, but they realized that he was healed through a divine power. They were right about that—Paul's understanding of the one God, divine Spirit, had healed him. ■

Read
a testimony related to this healing on page 254, "No Harm from Fire Ant Stings."

ISAIAH 41:10

"Fear thou not; for I am with thee: be not dismayed; for I am thy God: I will strengthen thee; yea, I will help thee."

Paul's great faith in God made him strong and fearless. Even a wild storm, a shipwreck, and a poisonous snake couldn't stop him from trusting God. He understood that God was with him—keeping him safe every moment. Paul knew deep down that God would help him no matter what happened. We can be like Paul and face scary times with trust in God. We can feel God's love all around us—no matter what situation we're in.

ACTS 28:7–10

PAUL HEALS PUBLIUS' FATHER OF ILLNESS

When Paul was being taken to Rome as a prisoner,  the boat carrying him was shipwrecked. But he and the others onboard made it safely to the island of Melita. There, he was healed of a snakebite.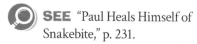

The ruler of the island was a man named Publius. He was kind to Paul and his friends Luke and Aristarchus, and he invited them to stay at his house for three days.

SEE Roman Empire, p. 281.

SEE "Paul Heals Himself of Snakebite," p. 231.

The Bible says that this man was sick of "a fever and of a bloody flux" (Acts 28:8). This meant that he suffered from a serious stomach disease.

SEE Healing by Touch, p. 267.

To find more information on color-coded terms, see pages 261–282.

CONCEPTS | CUSTOMS | GLOSSARY | PEOPLE | PLACES

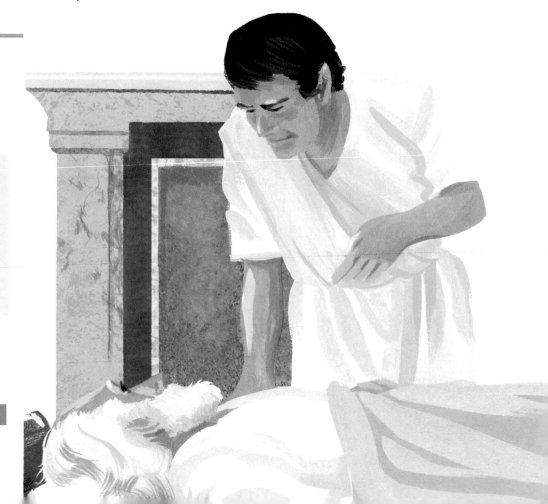

During this same time, Publius' father was very sick.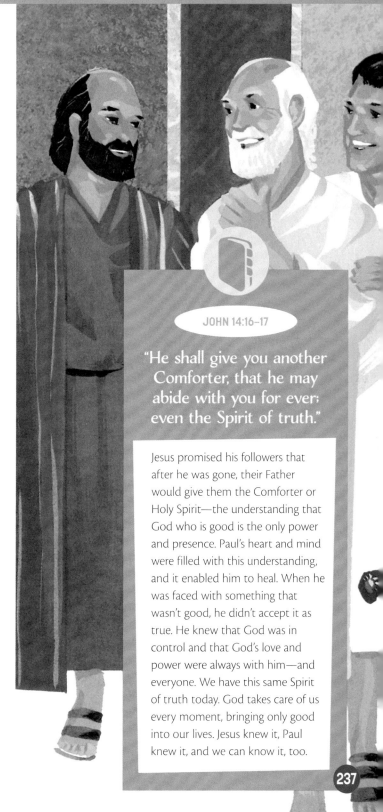

Paul was filled with the **Holy Spirit**—with the spiritual understanding of God's power. So he was always ready to help and heal—just as **Christ** Jesus had been. Paul went to this man and prayed. He also put his hand on him, which must have made him feel loved and cared for. Paul knew that this man was God's child—perfect, spiritual, and healthy. And he knew God kept him that way. Right away, the man was healed. He must have been so happy to be well again!

The news of this wonderful healing spread quickly around the island. Soon all the other sick people on the island of Melita were coming to Paul for help—and they were healed, too! For the next three months, Paul and his shipmates stayed on the island. Paul probably spent most of that time telling the islanders about Jesus' life and teachings and healing those who were sick.

Later, when Paul and his shipmates had found a different ship to use and were ready to leave for Rome,

JOHN 14:16–17

"He shall give you another Comforter, that he may abide with you for ever; even the Spirit of truth."

Jesus promised his followers that after he was gone, their Father would give them the Comforter or Holy Spirit—the understanding that God who is good is the only power and presence. Paul's heart and mind were filled with this understanding, and it enabled him to heal. When he was faced with something that wasn't good, he didn't accept it as true. He knew that God was in control and that God's love and power were always with him—and everyone. We have this same Spirit of truth today. God takes care of us every moment, bringing only good into our lives. Jesus knew it, Paul knew it, and we can know it, too.

the islanders gave Paul many supplies. They made sure that he and the others had everything they needed for the trip. This was a great way to show their love and gratitude for this great apostle who had taught them a new way to think and live and heal. Think what it meant to them to learn that the Holy Spirit—the understanding of God's all-power—was within them, too! ■

What can YOU do?

Have you ever felt unhappy about something in your life and thought you couldn't do anything about it? If so, remember Paul. He was a prisoner of the Romans. The ship he was on was shipwrecked, a snake bit him, and then he was stranded on an island. But no matter how bad things were, he knew that God loved him and always took care of him. You can know God loves you, too. Wherever you are, whatever has happened to you, you are never alone. God will help you and comfort you. Nothing is impossible with God's help!

HEALINGS *from* TODAY

The testimonies shared here prove that the same type of spiritual healing that occurred in Jesus' time happens today. Recognizing God's all-power plays a big part in these healings, along with gaining a better understanding of one's true nature as a child of God. Joy and gratitude are key elements, too—gratitude for God's loving care and happiness for the spiritual growth that is an important outcome of every healing.

These testimonies were first published in *The Christian Science Journal* or *Christian Science Sentinel*. Many of them have been shortened in order to include them in this book. If you'd like to read the whole thing, you can see where to find it at the beginning of each testimony.

Some of these are by children; others are by adults. The challenges healed range from speech, hearing, and skin problems to major injuries and paralysis.

Enjoy seeing how these individuals put into practice the same spiritual laws that made Jesus the greatest healer who ever lived.

A Daughter's Healing

FROM THE JANUARY 2020 ISSUE OF *THE CHRISTIAN SCIENCE JOURNAL*

Our youngest daughter has always been full of tremendous energy. However, one day when she was six years old, she became very lethargic. My husband and I soon noticed that she was having difficulty breathing and quickly hired a Christian Science practitioner to provide Christian Science treatment. We both had a lifetime of significant healings in Christian Science and felt confident in this choice of treatment for our daughter.

As my husband and I took turns holding our daughter close, we diligently prayed for her and felt the loving support of the practitioner, who I talked to several times about our daughter's progress. Here's what I knew: that God is All-Life and all-powerful; there is no opposing power that can take away the life or health of God's children; every child is a constant reflection of divine Life; my daughter has an inseparable relation to her true Father-Mother God.

I felt impelled to step out of the apartment for a short time to continue praying while my daughter rested in the capable arms of my husband, a Christian Science nurse.

My trust in God had frequently wavered. I had no problem acknowledging God's presence and harmonious effect in my life when life seemed good, but faith had become conditional for me. Now I prayed with all my heart to understand that God was, and is, always present and the only power; to know that no matter what appeared to be going on at that moment to the contrary, God was, in fact, governing our daughter and maintaining her health. I recognized that she couldn't for a moment be separated from God's loving care.

A tremendous joy and lightheartedness welled up in me. Every thought that had been nurturing fear dissolved entirely in the light of spiritual understanding. I headed back to the apartment to witness and celebrate my daughter's healing—what I was certain was her freedom from all symptoms of sickness.

When I stepped into the apartment, my husband was still holding my daughter, and it appeared that her condition had not changed at all. I refused to question the spiritual confidence I had gained. I denied the opportunity for fear or discouragement to sneak back in for even one second; I stood firmly on the side of Truth and insisted aloud that my daughter was whole, and that God was governing. Within a minute, she sat up, hopped off my husband's lap, and went about the evening as though she had never been ill. Every sign of sickness was gone, and she was back to her happy, active self.

My gratitude is boundless for this precious experience and the powerful lessons learned.

Angela Denson
Ballwin, Missouri, USA

Skin Eruption Cleared

FROM THE MAY 4, 2015 ISSUE OF THE *CHRISTIAN SCIENCE SENTINEL*

Some years ago an ugly skin eruption appeared on my face and wouldn't go away. I tried to keep my face clean and avoided touching it, as it appeared the condition was spreading. Because it seemed serious, an official at my school advised my parents and me that I should stay home.

While at home, I prayed each day over the next week. During that time I made progress in seeing that my true spiritual identity was never touched by evil of any kind. The major turning point came when I found this passage in the Bible: "If thou prepare thine heart, and stretch out thine hands toward him; if iniquity be in thine hand, put it far away, and let not wickedness dwell in thy tabernacles. For then shalt thou lift up thy face without spot" (Job 11:13–15).

I started reasoning from the fact that because God is Truth, God is without error or spot. And because God is without spot, I must also be without any kind of spot, or error.

When I affirmed that God's perfection also applied to me as God's child, the fear about the appearance of my face started to ebb.

Up to that point I had been using an antiseptic cleanser on my face. Through prayer, I discerned that I had been secretly hoping that this cleaning agent might remedy the skin condition. However, when I realized that this mixture of reliance on both matter and Spirit was delaying the healing, I stopped using the antiseptic and acknowledged that God is the only power. I saw that the skin eruption was nothing but an eruption of fear—a fearful belief that I could be outside of God's care.

I had learned in Sunday School that fear is an illusion—a belief of mortal mind that cannot be real, because God is the only Mind. I became convinced that my true identity is not a material physique but entirely spiritual, the reflection of God, Spirit, which could not be damaged. In reality, I was pure, whole, good—spotless.

After I had this change in thinking, the skin condition cleared quickly, for which I'm very grateful. An additional blessing was that people at my school noticed the change and wanted to know what had healed me. This gave me opportunities to share Christian Science with my friends and classmates.

Tad Blake-Weber
Waltham, Massachusetts, USA

My Victory over Childhood Paralysis

FROM THE DECEMBER 6, 2004 ISSUE OF THE *CHRISTIAN SCIENCE SENTINEL*

Just after I started school at the age of six, I became paralyzed from the waist down. I was required to be in a hospital, in a ward for those considered incurable. During this time, I was given no medication because the doctors did not know what was wrong with me and were worried that medication could make things worse. I was grateful for this, since I was praying to God as my only help in this situation.

I prayed to understand that all of God's children are truly His perfect creation, as the Bible states in the first chapter of Genesis, and that this applied to me as much as to all the other children in that ward. Because being unable to move was not good—was not like God's nature—I knew I did not have to accept it as true of me. I held with all my heart to the ideas that I had been taught in Christian Science Sunday School, which came to mind as I prayed.

After five weeks, I was lying in bed by the door to the ward, with my mother visiting me, when the hospital's chief consultant came through. He came back when he saw my mother and told her how sorry he was, but that nothing could be done for me. I was incurable and would be in a wheelchair all my life, paralyzed from the waist down.

I tugged at my mother's hand and pleaded with her to ask the consultant if I could seek help from a Christian Science practitioner. The consultant wanted to know what I was saying. My mother told him, and he replied that of course they knew that Christian Science cured things like colds, etc., but that this condition was incurable and I should not be given false hopes. However, he continued, if it helped comfort me, by all means we should seek help from a Christian Science practitioner. He then said, "In fact, why are we keeping your daughter in hospital now, when we can do no more for her?" An ambulance took me home, and I was carried to my bed.

My mother called a practitioner. She said she would pray for me. I went to sleep that night, feeling God was showing me that He was in control of this situation. I knew that I would be back to normal.

The following morning I awoke and jumped out of bed. My mother came in just then and was speechless. I asked if I could play in the yard. She happily agreed. I remember enjoying the beautiful sunny day, the butterflies, and the flowers.

The following year at school we had a medical examination, something that occurred every two years. I was a bit nervous before I saw the doctor, thinking he might find something still wrong with me. So I thought about how God is the divine Mind, and that we can only know what He knows about His creation.

After an hour-long examination, the doctor said he could not understand why I was completely well, given what he saw in my medical record. So he then gave me a further hour's examination. At the end, he said I was perfect and that this must be a miracle because there was no other explanation.

I was, and am, grateful that the "miracle" the doctors saw was no miracle to God.

Phyllis Woodhead
Claygate, Surrey, England

Epilepsy Healed

FROM THE NOVEMBER 18, 2013 ISSUE OF THE *CHRISTIAN SCIENCE SENTINEL*

Before I came to know Christian Science, I suffered from epilepsy for more than seven years. I sought treatment from doctors, but they told me that it was a chronic ailment and that they had no cure beyond medicine to manage the seizures. Since I could have a seizure at any time, my family kept me at home so they could keep an eye on me. I was told that because of my condition I could never drive, ride a bicycle, climb trees, or go near fire. My life was that of a slave.

One day about five years ago, I was searching for a religion that offered some hope of restoring my health. I found claims that Christian Science heals. I searched more deeply and found a lot of talk about the book *Science and Health with Key to the Scriptures* by Mary Baker Eddy—a book that heals! I started reading it, and although it was hard for me to understand it, I went on reading.

One passage that really stood out to me was this one: "Discerning the rights of man, we cannot fail to foresee the doom of all oppression. Slavery is not the legitimate state of man. God made man free. Paul said, 'I was free born.' All men should be free. 'Where the Spirit of the Lord is, there is liberty'" (p. 227). I started to see that I couldn't be kept in slavery by epilepsy, and that this "oppression" didn't come from God.

Over the next several years, I continued to receive guidance from *Science and Health*, together with the Bible. I started to see that disease was a form of mortal mind, or animal magnetism (see *Science and Health*, p. 178)—which was really nothing but a belief that life could exist in matter instead of in God, Spirit. In other words, epilepsy is nothing but the image of a lie.

As I felt the truth of these concepts, I was healed. I had no more seizures, and I rode a bicycle for the first time since I had been diagnosed with epilepsy. I returned to the clinic soon after, and the doctors confirmed my healing.

I have found health and harmony in my life, and thanks to Christian Science I know how to overcome various beliefs of error. Jesus promised, "Ye shall know the truth, and the truth shall make you free" (John 8:32). I am so grateful to be free now!

Fredy J. Kaganda
Nyarugusu Camp,
Kasulu, Tanzania

Healing Following a Fall

FROM THE MAY 29, 2000 ISSUE OF THE *CHRISTIAN SCIENCE SENTINEL*

The catwalk on which I was standing in a building under construction suddenly gave way. Plummeting from the top floor through the lower levels of the building, I landed on the concrete basement floor more than fifty feet below. No one was there, and no one was within earshot to hear my cries for help. As I lay there, however, collecting my thoughts, I began to feel that God was present.

I had, as was usual for me, begun my day studying the Bible and correlative passages from *Science and Health with Key to the Scriptures* by Mary Baker Eddy as found in the *Christian Science Quarterly* Weekly Bible Lessons. As I lay there on the basement floor, I clung to what I'd gained that morning about God's protecting presence and power.

Paul's words to the believers in Philippi held special significance at that moment: "The Lord is at hand. . . . In every thing by prayer and supplication with thanksgiving let your requests be made known unto God. . . . God shall supply all your need according to his riches in glory by Christ Jesus" (Phil. 4:5–6, 19).

These were the unshaken convictions of a man who had experienced all kinds of difficulties, including life-threatening situations. Beaten, stoned, arrested on false charges, shipwrecked, attacked by a venomous snake, imprisoned, he spoke about God's care from firsthand experience.

I reasoned that if Almighty God is indeed "at hand," then the power to meet my need was both immediate and ever present. Another statement by Paul also took on greater significance: "I am persuaded, that neither death, nor life, nor angels, nor principalities, nor powers, nor things present, nor things to come, nor height, nor depth, nor any other creature, shall be able to separate us from the love of God, which is in Christ Jesus our Lord" (Rom. 8:38–39).

It was comforting to realize that I couldn't be separated from God's love by height or depth, that no power in the present or the future could deprive me of God's presence, and that God's love for me and all His children couldn't be jeopardized by an accident, even one that appeared serious. I was claiming my uninterrupted relation to God, my real, spiritual identity made in God's image and likeness, which is never subject to accidents or danger.

Uplifted, I actually felt grateful for this opportunity to prove man's unbroken relation to God, instead of viewing it as a calamity. I soon emerged from the basement unharmed, joyous, completely free of any injury.

Clifford Kapps Eriksen
Saint James, New York, USA

Honesty Is the Only Policy

FROM THE MARCH 21, 1994 ISSUE OF THE *CHRISTIAN SCIENCE SENTINEL*

"If any man be in Christ, he is a new creature: old things are passed away; behold, all things are become new" (II Cor. 5:17). This statement from the Bible has certainly been proved true to me. Through the study of Christian Science, I've been transformed from being a dishonest person to an honest one.

I was desperately seeking a job. Upon completing an application, an interviewer called me to ask why I hadn't entered any work history. I stated honestly that I had no prior work experience to speak of. He replied, "Well, we're going to have to doctor your résumé." This was a moment of decision for me. "Sir, put the facts exactly as I've stated," I firmly countered. There was a time when I would have gone along with a scheme to falsify my résumé; but because I had since grown spiritually, I found such a course of action unacceptable.

I continued my job search. During an interview I was again asked why my application was blank. I explained that, quite honestly, I had rarely held a steady job. The interviewer described briefly what the job entailed and the skills required to do the job. I said I had no experience in this type of work, but I quickly added that I was willing to learn. After further discussion, he said he would consider my application.

One passage I had pondered while searching for work was written by Mary Baker Eddy: "The devotion of thought to an honest achievement makes the achievement possible. Exceptions only confirm this rule, proving that failure is occasioned by a too feeble faith" (*Science and Health with Key to the Scriptures*, p. 199). I knew I had to be completely candid about my past, and my faith in God was growing daily.

With these points in mind, I felt very confident that God would lead me to the right job.

The next evening I received a call from the man who had interviewed me, asking me to report to work the next morning. I arrived promptly at 8:30 and began the job. I've been working for this company for nine years, and am considered one of its top mechanics.

Whenever I'm in need of inspiration, I recall how God provided me with a job when it appeared I would be completely unable to find one. In a world where it appears that doing dishonest deeds often aids in advancement, my experience has proved that, by being honest, you will be justly rewarded by our heavenly Father. It's been said that "Honesty is the best policy," for me, "Honesty is the *only* policy."

Louis Fuentes
New York, New York, USA

Seeing Clearly

FROM THE MARCH 11, 2019 ISSUE OF THE *CHRISTIAN SCIENCE SENTINEL*

I was in the car with my mom, who was driving me to a volleyball tournament, when suddenly I found myself having trouble seeing. There were large black spots in my left eye, and they seemed to grow larger until it became almost impossible to see out of that eye. At first I told myself that whatever was wrong would just go away. But as I closed my eyes, it occurred to me that, actually, I could pray about the issue as I'd learned in the Christian Science Sunday School, because in the past, prayer had helped me with other problems.

I also told my mom what was going on, because I was afraid and wanted her to help me pray. She helped me shift my perspective to a more spiritual one by sharing the spiritual definition of *eyes* from the Glossary of *Science and Health with Key to the Scriptures* by Mary Baker Eddy. While most of us might think of eyes simply as two physical organs, it helped to consider them differently, and I listened as my mom shared the definition: "EYES. Spiritual discernment,—not material but mental." The definition continues, "Jesus said, thinking of the outward vision, 'Having eyes, see ye not?'" (p. 586).

I reasoned that since God is Spirit, and everything God made is spiritual, then my sight is spiritual, too, and I felt a little more confident about my true vision being permanent.

After we prayed with these ideas for a while, I felt less afraid. I thought of what an early student of Christian Science remembered Mary Baker Eddy saying about healing instantaneously: "I will tell you the way to do it. It is to love! Just live love—be it—love, love, love. Do not know anything but Love. Be all love. There is nothing else. That will do the work" (*We Knew Mary Baker Eddy*, expanded edition, vol. I, pp. 296–297). She wasn't just talking about being a really nice and loving person, but about feeling and expressing the love that comes from God, divine Love.

As I thought about this, a warm, fuzzy feeling of love began to flood my thoughts, and despite my discomfort, I forgot about my eye. I started to focus on loving everything and everyone I saw around me. I began to express gratitude for literally everything that was visible to me. I realized how easy it had become for me to love all the people I saw, because this love came from God, and God created us as His loved sons and daughters—brothers and sisters. I saw loving them as a completely normal thing to do.

Before I knew it, the large black spots in my eye had dissolved completely. When I saw the world around me through my spiritual vision, in the light of divine Love, the healing took place.

I was able to play volleyball really well that day and to have a great tournament.

Emmi Easton
Ballwin, Missouri, USA

Vision Restored after Eye Injury

FROM THE MARCH 2020 ISSUE OF *THE CHRISTIAN SCIENCE JOURNAL*

One day last summer I was on a path along a creek bed, normally a pleasant and inspiring walk to watch the sunrise. But when I bent a bush out of my way, one of the branches snapped back and poked me directly in the center of my eye. My sight went dark immediately in that eye—the eye that's most important in my work as an architectural and fine art photographer.

On page 397 of *Science and Health with Key to the Scriptures*, Mary Baker Eddy writes:

> When an accident happens, you think or exclaim, 'I am hurt!' Your thought is more powerful than your words, more powerful than the accident itself, to make the injury real.

> Now reverse the process. Declare that you are not hurt and understand the reason why, and you will find the ensuing good effects to be in exact proportion to your disbelief in physics, and your fidelity to divine metaphysics, confidence in God as All, which the Scriptures declare Him to be.

I reasoned that sight does not come from material eyes made up of muscles, lenses, and retinas. True sight is the spiritual perception each of us has as the expression of the all-knowing and all-seeing divine Mind. And since Mind never loses sight of the goodness of its ideas, neither can we as Mind's perfect spiritual reflection lose sight of our own or others' spiritual perfection.

The sight in that eye returned immediately. But what was even more awe-inspiring is that my vision was even clearer than it had been before.

The lesson I have taken away from this experience is the importance of confidently and fearlessly declaring the perfection of God's man, regardless of material appearances. Mentally replacing the false, mortal view with what we know to be spiritually true brings healing. And the more we do this, the easier it becomes.

Robert Hansen
Laguna Niguel, California, USA

Surrounded by Love at Camp

FROM THE JULY 2, 2007 ISSUE OF THE *CHRISTIAN SCIENCE SENTINEL*

A few summers ago, I was a counselor at a summer camp for Christian Scientists.

One evening, my cabin of six middle-school-aged girls went bumper tubing on the lake—a water sport where you ride in a tube that's attached by a rope to a powerboat. After everyone had had a turn, my co-counselor and I decided to take a ride together.

After about five seconds of pulling us along, the rope became tangled and I flew off my tube, hitting the water awkwardly and forcefully. Immediately I realized that I couldn't do anything but float on my back and move my fingers just a little bit. Fear swept over me.

My co-counselor swam over and began to reassure me that I could never be outside of God's care. Divine Love was holding me and caring for me. I held to the idea that I didn't have to accept this situation as the reality of my spiritual being. These ideas were familiar to me since I'd learned through experiences in my life that prayer heals. Rather than feeling scared, I felt calm enough to pray and keep my thoughts focused on God. Within minutes, I wasn't afraid anymore.

I was taken to shore, and the camp's Christian Science nurses, practitioner, and director were all there to assist me. The director informed me that my parents had been notified and had begun to support me through prayer.

While I knew I could receive medical help if I wanted it, I expected healing through prayer. So I chose to be taken to the camp's care facility, where I'd receive Christian Science nursing care. When I arrived, the Christian Science nurse on duty helped me get ready for bed. The camp practitioner was there too, quietly sharing prayerful ideas. After about half an hour of just holding on to the thought of God's love, I was able to sit up, stand, and walk slowly with support. That night, I fell asleep feeling safe, fearless, and confident of a complete healing.

However, the next morning I woke up in pain and felt frustrated because my ability to walk and move around normally was limited.

I knew I'd made a lot of progress the night before, but a gloomy cloud had settled on my thoughts. In that moment, I realized that similar feelings of negativity and frustration had been bugging me at camp that summer, on a daily basis. And as a result, my whole attitude, and sometimes behavior, had been poor. The steady peace that I normally associated with camp hadn't been present in my thoughts or in my experience.

Since I was so distracted by these negative feelings, I knew it would be difficult to pray for healing without first addressing the gloomy thoughts and adjusting my attitude about camp. As I humbly asked for divine guidance, I realized that when I focused on what was wrong with my camp experience, just like with my body, I wasn't awake to harmony, which comes from God and is constantly available.

I came across these passages from *Unity of Good*: "All that is beautiful and good in your individual consciousness is permanent. That which is not so is illusive and fading. . . . Look up, not down, for your fields are already white for the harvest" (p. 8, pp. 11–12).

From my room in the care facility, I was able to experience God's love. Just outside my open window, I saw the patience of a counselor tirelessly teaching a small boy how to serve a tennis ball; the cheering of kids as they congratulated a friend for getting a bull's eye in archery; and the enthusiasm of campers learning how to play the drums in rhythmic unison. Camp was *overflowing* with joy and love!

That afternoon, I remember feeling eager to get back to my campers and my duties as a counselor. Getting out of myself, and focusing on all the good that was being demonstrated, I couldn't wait to express this love myself. The change in my thought was so liberating that I totally forgot about my body. I steadily walked into the other room to share my inspiration with the Christian Science nurse—very conscious of my spiritual selfhood and indestructible connection to God.

I left the care facility that night with very little discomfort, and a very large sense of my purpose at camp—to actively express the Love that was always present. The following day, I spent more quiet time in gratitude and prayer, and was able to continue with my normal camp activities, including sailing.

Within the next week, all residual aches and pains completely dissolved. For the rest of the summer, I felt joyful and genuinely grateful to be at camp. But best of all, I had learned how opening my eyes to a spiritual perspective can bring healing to every challenging situation.

Heather Harmon
(now Heather Goldsmith)
Hingham, Massachusetts, USA

Claim Your True Inheritance

FROM THE AUG. 18, 2014 ISSUE OF THE *CHRISTIAN SCIENCE SENTINEL*

I began studying Christian Science over 25 years ago. At that time I was dealing with some physical challenges.

I'd been suffering from migraines for several years, an ailment that I supposedly had inherited from members of my family, as well as from a frequent sore throat, a condition my mother often had.

We learn in Christian Science that we are the children of our heavenly Father-Mother God and can be heirs only to everything that is good. Mary Baker Eddy writes, "Heredity is a prolific subject for mortal belief to pin theories upon; but if we learn that nothing is real but the right, we shall have no dangerous inheritances, and fleshly ills will disappear" (*Science and Health with Key to the Scriptures*, p. 228).

In Christian Science prayer consists of replacing false beliefs with spiritual truths about God and man. Doing this radically changes our thinking. I've learned that it's important to take a stand and firmly recognize that, as the Apostle Paul said, "we live, and move, and have our being" (Acts 17:28) in divine Spirit. This means we are constantly in the abundance of infinite good, and we should be watchful and always aware of our divine inheritance.

This spiritual understanding also helped me see very clearly that people don't inherit a disease, harmful habits, or difficult character traits from their relatives. Our heritage is divine, and we can inherit only good, harmony, and health.

These ideas helped free me from migraines and sore throats, and they completely dissolved any fear of inheriting a disease.

Laura Victoria Rojas
Bogotá, Colombia

Speech Difficulty Healed

FROM THE JANUARY 15, 1990 ISSUE OF THE *CHRISTIAN SCIENCE SENTINEL*

Our younger daughter was in tears because no one in our family could understand what she was saying. We knew that she had lost something from her pocket—something that was precious to her. I prayed with a desire to help her, something our family needed to do often when communicating with this child. We longed to have her healed of a serious speech difficulty. In my prayers for her, I realized that everyone with challenging speech difficulties could experience freedom. It was comforting to have faith that one's inclusive prayers would bless our child and others.

Ever since she had begun to talk, most of the time we could only guess at what she was saying. As a Christian Scientist, I knew that the beauty and perfection of God were expressed by our child in her true being, the spiritual image of God. This divine fact had to be proved through practice of the spiritual truths that the Bible and Christian Science teach.

As I prayed to help our daughter find what she had lost, I noticed a small book with a cover that portrayed a noted author and her daughter. I then asked our daughter if she was telling us that she had lost a picture of a little girl hugging her mother. She happily nodded yes. Her tears changed to smiles when she finally received the longed-for answer and the picture.

At bedtime our two daughters prayed the following prayer for children by Mary Baker Eddy:

Father-Mother God,
　Loving me,—
Guard me when I sleep;
Guide my little feet
　Up to Thee.

(*Miscellaneous Writings 1883–1896*, p. 400)

After our younger daughter listened to her sister say the prayer, she could only say in broken English, "I pray the same, God." We knew she longed to speak as well as her sister and the other little children.

A statement from *Science and Health* is engraved on the wall of many branch churches: "Divine Love always has met and always will meet every human need." My family and I considered deeply and reverently this sacred promise with its power to heal.

My mother was coming to lunch one day when we were praying with strong trust that divine Love does "meet every human need." As my mother entered our house, she asked, "Can Patricia speak any better?" In a little while, as we gathered around the dining table, our younger daughter greatly pleased us as she said perfectly, "I can say *God*; I can say *good*; I can say *Love*; I can say anything at all." And she could! Our family was profoundly grateful for this beautiful healing of speech.

In kindergarten and first grade our younger daughter's school marks had been poor. In second grade, after her healing of defective speech, she received all A's. Her teacher wrote to my husband and me saying that in all her years of teaching she had never known such a remarkable improvement in a student's speech. She called the marvelous turnaround a miracle.

When this daughter was in high school, her school chose her to represent them in a television program because of her excellent speaking and confident manner. Regarding the healing of speech, I recall this hymn in the *Hymnal*:

It was the voice of God that spake
  In silence to thy silent heart,
And bade each worthier thought awake,
  And every dream of earth depart.

(Stephen G. Bulfinch, hymn 94)

Louisa Velnett Palmer
Kent, Ohio, USA

Healed of Back Pain

FROM THE JULY 2012 ISSUE OF *THE CHRISTIAN SCIENCE JOURNAL*

I am grateful for a marvelous healing I experienced about two years ago.

When I woke up one morning, I had in some way hurt my back, and it was very difficult to move without severe pain. I declared that as God's child, I was spiritual and had dominion over matter and that I was created in "His image and likeness" (*Science and Health*, p. 468; see Genesis 1:26). I've always found that the healing truths of the Bible are an ever-present help in times of need. After praying for more than an hour, I was able to take a shower.

I was claiming my perfection as a child of God, and as I stepped out of the shower, these words of Jesus came into my thinking: "Woman, thou art loosed from thine infirmity" (Luke 13:12).

That was what Jesus said to the woman who had been bound for 18 years. And like her, my thought was transformed and I was immediately healed. The same healing power that was with that woman over 2,000 years ago was with me in that moment.

The pain just disappeared! I was in awe because I was healed in the amount of time it took to lift my foot out of the shower and onto the bath mat. I have never had any back pain since.

I was in such awe of the healing presence of the Christ. I'm still in awe today. How blessed we are in Christian Science to be able to bear witness to the healing power of the Christ.

Jean Bell
Balgownie, New South Wales,
Australia

251

Daughter's Normal Hearing Restored

FROM THE JUNE 4, 2007 ISSUE OF THE *CHRISTIAN SCIENCE SENTINEL*

In June 2006, while my daughter, Emma, was in kindergarten, she took a standard hearing examination. Soon after this test, the school board of education contacted me, stating that Emma had been diagnosed with a hearing problem, affecting the functioning of her middle ear. They indicated that she would be retested in the coming school year.

As I thought about this, I realized there had been occasional times when my daughter wouldn't respond to my husband or me, particularly when we whispered or were speaking to her from a distance. But it had never occurred to us that this indicated a hearing problem.

The results of this hearing test gave me the opportunity to pray about this in Christian Science. I knew prayer could heal this, just as it had many other challenges we'd faced as a family.

In my prayers, I decided to look into Christ Jesus' healings in the Bible, as well as the many instructive statements of spiritual truth in *Science and Health with Key to the Scriptures*. Both of these books were full of evidence that my child's hearing could definitely be restored.

In the Bible, I read of a deaf man brought to Jesus for healing. According to the account, Jesus put his fingers into the man's ears. "And looking up to heaven, he sighed, and saith unto him, Ephphatha, that is, Be opened. And straightway his ears were opened" (see Mark 7:32–37). I knew that the same power that restored this man's hearing—the living, healing Christ—was available for my daughter. Then I read the following statement in *Science and Health*: "Sight, hearing, all the spiritual senses of man, are eternal. They cannot be lost" (p. 486).

After praying with these truths, my fear and concern disappeared. I had complete trust that my daughter was well and that we could expect to see healing.

Very soon my husband and I began to notice that Emma could hear us more consistently in all situations. Also, whereas she'd once been extremely shy, she was now more outgoing and playful.

I'd actually forgotten about the hearing retest until I received a notice in the mail. Emma had been retested, and the new results indicated that her hearing was normal and that she wouldn't need to be tested again. On the form, indicating the functioning of the child's middle ear, the testers had scratched out "improved" and handwritten the word "good." I found this especially noteworthy, since it was evidence of the permanent spiritual fact laid down in Genesis, that God created everything and "it was very good" (1:31).

Through prayer in Christian Science, it became clear to me that Emma's hearing couldn't be anything other than good. And that's what we saw.

Debra Chew
Knoxville, Tennessee, USA

Ankle Injury Healed

FROM THE AUGUST 8, 2016 ISSUE OF THE *CHRISTIAN SCIENCE SENTINEL*

I am so grateful for the immediate help I recently received through prayer and Christian Science treatment. I had spent all day walking in a large city, and at the end of the day I needed to take a bus to another large city. Upon arriving in this other city, I was planning to walk to a friend's house.

During the day, I sustained an injury to my ankle, which caused considerable discomfort. When I got on the bus for the two-hour ride, I was in great pain and couldn't put any weight on my foot.

I prayed for much of the bus trip, silently affirming "the scientific statement of being" from *Science and Health with Key to the Scriptures* by Mary Baker Eddy, which begins: "There is no life, truth, intelligence, nor substance in matter. All is infinite Mind and its infinite manifestation, for God is All-in-all" (p. 468).

It was clear to me that as much as it might seem that the world is governed by material laws, God's spiritual laws actually govern the entire universe, including each one of us, showing that so-called material laws are not really laws, but beliefs.

Just as the bus was about to approach my stop, words from the New Testament glimmered in my consciousness: "And immediately his feet and ankle bones received strength" (Acts 3:7). These words are included in the story of Peter healing a beggar who couldn't walk. I was amazed by how the early Christian healers didn't view healing as a drawn-out process, but instead as an instantaneous response to the realization that life is spiritual, not material.

I was humbled that the God from Bible times is the same God right now and forever. God is the same power, authority, and lawmaker today as He was then and always will be.

The bus pulled up to my stop. I stood up and walked normally without experiencing any pain. I was so grateful to be healed through Christian Science. The ankle has been fine ever since.

Shelly Richardson
Eugene, Oregon, USA

No Harm from Fire Ant Stings

FROM THE JUNE 13, 2016 ISSUE OF THE *CHRISTIAN SCIENCE SENTINEL*

Our family had an unforgettable proof of the healing power of divine Love when we were living in Texas some years ago. Our six-year-old daughter was out in the backyard playing when I suddenly heard her screaming. I rushed out and found her standing in the middle of a fire ant nest. Countless excited ants were crawling on her feet and ankles and stinging her.

I removed her from the nest, turned on the hose full blast, and quickly washed the ants away. Then I carried her into the house and did my best to comfort her. Her body started swelling up. I was afraid and called a Christian Science practitioner and asked her to pray.

As I was holding my daughter and praying, Paul's experience with the viper came to mind (see Acts 28:1–5). When onlookers saw that he had been bitten by the viper, they felt sure he must be an evil man because this harm had come upon him. But Paul simply shook off the viper. The bite didn't hurt him.

All at once I felt a sense of relief. Joy came over me as I realized that just as Paul was innocent of any wrongdoing, so was my daughter—she'd had no intention of disturbing the fire ants' home. I wasn't afraid anymore and knew my daughter was completely safe in God's all-embracing presence.

She fell asleep for about 15 minutes, and when she woke up, she was peaceful. The swelling in her body completely disappeared in a couple of hours. The omnipotent government of divine Love had nullified any material belief that one of God's creatures could injure another. Mary Baker Eddy writes on page 514 of *Science and Health with Key to the Scriptures*: "Understanding the control which Love held over all, Daniel felt safe in the lions' den, and Paul proved the viper to be harmless. All of God's creatures, moving in the harmony of Science, are harmless, useful, indestructible."

Helen Farmer
Wheat Ridge, Colorado, USA

254

Victory over Death

FROM THE AUGUST 2010 ISSUE OF *THE CHRISTIAN SCIENCE JOURNAL*

Years ago, I had an experience that helped me see something of what Mary Baker Eddy is saying about life and death in the following quote from *Science and Health with Key to the Scriptures*:

> One moment of divine consciousness, or the spiritual understanding of Life and Love, is a foretaste of eternity. This exalted view, obtained and retained when the Science of being is understood, would bridge over with life discerned spiritually the interval of death, and man would be in the full consciousness of his immortality and eternal harmony, where sin, sickness, and death are unknown. (p. 598)

This moment of "divine consciousness" came one day when I was at home. I heard people crying in a building next door, and I decided to go see what was going on. A man had just been pronounced dead by a doctor. I felt impelled to ask the family for permission to see the man alone. It was evident there was no sign of life. Immediately I began to pray to God and became aware that the infinite life that God gives us transcends the false, mortal concept that life begins and ends. I was completely conscious that this was the only truth about everyone, including this man. I understood that our real individuality is spiritual, in divine Life itself, and couldn't be destroyed by death. Within a few minutes, the man got up by himself and embraced me.

This was just one example to me of how it's possible to raise the dead today through the revelation of Christian Science.

José de Dios Mata
Madrid, Spain

Grateful to God

FROM THE NOV. 26, 2012 ISSUE OF THE *CHRISTIAN SCIENCE SENTINEL*

One day in the evening, I went to a park with my mother and my younger brother, Tarun. When I was playing on the swings I lost my grip and fell down. I was in great pain. My mother helped me to stand up as I was not able to stand straight. She prayed with me and talked to me about my true spiritual self that is the image of God. She said I am a son of God and "not made up of brain, blood, bones," as it says in the book *Science and Health with Key to the Scriptures* by Mary Baker Eddy (p. 475). Nothing bad can really happen to a son of God because God always protects His children. And God gives me strength.

After reaching home, I called a Christian Science practitioner to pray for me as I had a lot of pain. The practitioner told me that accidents are unreal because God does not know of them. God only knows good. In *Science and Health* it says that "there is no pain in Truth, and no truth in pain" (p. 113).

After that I was able to have my dinner. And then I sang Hymn 263 from the *Christian Science Hymnal* with my mother. The hymn starts, "Only God can bring us gladness, / Only God can give us peace." After that I went to bed and I slept peacefully. In the morning when I woke up there was a little pain. I reported this to the practitioner, and she told me to keep praying with the same truths we had talked about. And I did. The next morning I was totally free.

I am grateful to God for this wonderful healing.

Sahil
Chandigarh, India

Symptoms of Learning Disabilities Healed

FROM THE DECEMBER 2003 ISSUE OF *THE CHRISTIAN SCIENCE JOURNAL*

A few years ago, when my son was in second grade, his teacher told me he needed to be tested for learning disabilities. She suggested he had dyslexia because he reversed more letters than was typical for kids his age, and sometimes he reversed entire words. She also thought that he wasn't as focused as he should be and should be tested for Attention Deficit Disorder.

I left the meeting distressed. But I also realized that this was an opportunity for me to take a stand for who my son really was—the child of God, as I've learned through my study of Christian Science. I knew I had to see him as complete—not lacking in any ability to express God, who is infinite intelligence.

My husband and I decided to arrange for a reading tutor. I also contacted a Christian Science practitioner, who agreed to pray for him each day. The practitioner recommended that he take some time each day to read from the Bible and *Science and Health with Key to the Scriptures*. In addition, my son and I read and talked about many inspirational hymns.

All the while, I was praying for him, too, endeavoring to see my son as God's child. I knew that what was true for him was true for each of God's children.

Within a month, my son's reading took off. His handwriting improved a lot, and his word reversals entirely disappeared—as did most of his letter reversals. His tutor called me and said she was absolutely certain there was nothing wrong with my son and that we could end the tutoring. I felt this was evidence of something Mary Baker Eddy said in *Science and Health*, "the physical senses must give up their false testimony" (p. 192). I was grateful that my son's true, spiritual nature was coming to light.

The following year, my son's third grade teacher said he was so focused and worked so well with others that he could handle situations that were often difficult for other kids. And in fourth grade, he took a statewide test and scored in the highest level in nearly every subject.

Rondi A. Olson
Woodinville, Washington, USA

Cold Symptoms Disappear

FROM THE JULY 2019 ISSUE OF *THE CHRISTIAN SCIENCE JOURNAL*

A healing I experienced several years ago has been a staff for me to lean on. I had a severe cold. Unable to sleep, I propped myself up in bed, picked up a copy of the *Christian Science Sentinel*, and started reading.

One of the articles discussed Christ Jesus' healing of the man with the withered hand. Thinking about this story, I knew that when Jesus said, "Stretch forth thine hand" (Matthew 12:13), he was certain healing would take place and the man's hand would be made whole as the other because God, who is totally good and created all, did not create disease, deformity, or any other evil. Therefore evil could not, in reality, be included in man's being or experience. No matter how real the withered condition of a hand looked, it was not the reality.

Mary Baker Eddy, who discovered the spiritual sense of Jesus' teachings in her study of the Bible, wrote in *Science and Health with Key to the Scriptures*: "Look away from the body into Truth and Love, the Principle of all happiness, harmony, and immortality. Hold thought steadfastly to the enduring, the good, and the true, and you will bring these into your experience proportionably to their occupancy of your thoughts" (p. 261).

That was what I was doing. And as I was thinking about Jesus' complete confidence in God's healing ability, my nasal passages began to clear. I was skeptical at first that this could be happening so fast, since mortal thought argues that recovery from a cold takes time. But the cold cleared up quickly and effortlessly. The symptoms just disappeared into nothingness. Needless to say, I was very grateful!

Thalia Hutter
Chardon, Ohio, USA

Rash Healed

FROM THE APRIL 13, 2015 ISSUE OF THE *CHRISTIAN SCIENCE SENTINEL*

A few years ago when our youngest son was in high school, he remarked one morning before school that he had a rash of some kind on his stomach. Later that day he went to the school nurse's office to get a band-aid to cover the area. The nurse called me to say she had noticed that our son needed medical attention. I thanked her for her call and assured her we would take care of the issue.

At home that evening our son, my husband, and I talked about how we could pray to address this. Our son suggested we work with a statement he had recently studied in Christian Science Sunday School, "Spiritual sense, contradicting the material senses, involves intuition, hope, faith, understanding, fruition, reality" (Mary Baker Eddy, *Science and Health with Key to the Scriptures*, p. 298).

We could all see we needed to view the situation not with the material senses, which indicated a rash, but with our spiritual sense, which included the intuition, hope, faith, and understanding necessary to see clearly that God is the creator of man, and that the man of God's creating includes only innocence, purity, harmony, and health. This was the only condition our son could express. We all felt confident affirming this truth about God and man.

In a few days the rash was completely gone and had not caused our son any pain or inconvenience.

We are indeed grateful for our divine Father-Mother God's constant love and care and for all the lessons about God and man we gain through the study, application, and demonstration of Christian Science.

Blythe Evans
Scottsdale, Arizona, USA

When Our Son Was Hurt, We Turned to God

FROM THE FEBRUARY 2004 ISSUE OF *THE CHRISTIAN SCIENCE JOURNAL*

Our two teenage boys were skiing together that day. Around noon we heard our older son calling for us on his radio. His brother was seriously hurt, and we needed to come quickly to the terrain park. He missed the landing on a jump and, upon impact, hit his head.

We started to pray immediately. And we asked that a Christian Science practitioner pray with us. Almost at once, the tender message came to me that God, our Father-Mother, was with each one of us—right then. I also took comfort in knowing that the boys had a strong foundation for prayer from Sunday School and that they knew they could instantly turn to God for comfort and healing.

By the time we reached the terrain park, medics were on the scene. They had already called for an emergency helicopter and were preparing our son, who was unconscious, for an immediate airlift off the mountain. We would have to ski down the hill and drive for nearly an hour to join him at the hospital.

We arrived at the neurology critical care ward of the hospital where the head neurosurgeon on duty showed us CAT scan images of our son's head. The surgeon explained that he needed us to sign papers of release for immediate surgery, as our son was in a coma and the odds of his coming out of it were about 50 percent. In the surgeon's opinion, there was no other choice but to perform the surgery.

We asked for a few minutes to talk together privately. As we did this, it became clear to us that there *was* a choice, and that we could expect healing. We told the doctor that we would sign the papers and allow him to proceed with the surgery if it was, in fact, the only option. But we asked to be able to first spend 30 minutes with our child in undisturbed prayer. The doctor agreed to this.

We spent the next half hour talking to our son about his perfect, spiritual nature as the child of God. We talked about the twenty-third Psalm, reassuring him that he wasn't walking "through the valley of the shadow of death," that he had no evil to fear (Ps. 23:4). We went through the Lord's Prayer, and talked about how it applied to him directly (see Matt. 6:9–13). We spoke to him throughout that half hour, praying to know that our son wasn't really a material being, but the spiritual likeness of God, as the Bible says.

When the doctor returned to make "one last try" to rouse our son, he told us that the situation was stabilizing. He said he was willing to give us a little more time because he felt that our son was acting "purposeful." This word *purposeful* was something we really held to as we prayed throughout that night.

I decided to read *Science and Health with Key to the Scriptures* by Mary Baker Eddy, one page at a time, and let the words speak to me. And oh, they did!

At about three in the morning, these words about Jesus leaped off the page: "His purpose in healing was not alone to restore health, but to demonstrate his divine Principle. He was inspired by God, by Truth and Love, in all that he said and did." The marginal heading here read, "Example for our salvation" (*Science and Health*, p. 51). It was clear to me that I needed to be following Jesus' example—praying not just to restore my son's health, but to see the perfection of God's creation demonstrated.

I saw that, as a son of God, my son's true purpose was to reflect and express God. Because God is Life, it was right for my son to be an active thinker and doer. Because God is Mind, I knew that my son had to reflect this one all-knowing source of intelligence. And I knew that infinite intelligence was actually in control of everyone and everything. At six the next morning, the doctor returned, prepared to move ahead with the surgery. It was then that our son opened one eye.

Needless to say, we were extremely grateful. This improvement in our son's condition changed the doctors' view of the situation—they no longer felt the need to perform surgery. And after that, our son continued to get better.

We only spent four days in that hospital, rather than the many weeks the doctors had initially prepared us for. During that time, we continued to pray by our son's bedside 24 hours a day. The practitioner also prayed with us. Less than 24 hours after he came out of the coma, our son was out of bed and walking the hall with his dad. And four days later, our family flew home just as we'd originally planned.

The progress continued after we got home. We were in daily contact with the practitioner. I'd drive my son to the practitioner's office and the two of them would tackle prayer-based solutions to the issues that my son was still facing. And there were many. At first, he was paralyzed on one side of his body. He couldn't retain information from one day to the next. He couldn't even write his name. But one by one, every difficulty was addressed through prayer and healed.

Ten days after the incident, our son was back in school. And within a two-week period he was caught up in all of his classes and had reestablished a 3.83 grade point average. Now, one year later, our son continues to be an honors student in his high school. He's an avid soccer player, and he hasn't lost any of his enthusiasm for skiing.

Lyndi Sheasley
Bellevue, Washington, USA

Football Injury Healed

FROM THE AUGUST 6, 2009 ISSUE OF THE *CHRISTIAN SCIENCE SENTINEL*

Growing up in Texas, I started playing football in full pads in second grade. In my junior year, I started the first game of the varsity season against a former state championship team. It was a rather daunting experience for me, as I lined up across from a guy that outweighed me by nearly 100 pounds. Just a few plays into the game, he drove his helmet into the back of my exposed ankle—a cheap shot. After helping me up, he asked me if my leg hurt. I answered that it did, and he replied, "I'm going to break it." I was filled with feelings of fear, anger, confusion, and pain as I struggled to finish the first half of the game.

Whenever I'd faced a physical challenge or illness before, I'd always found healing through relying solely on Christian Science prayer-based treatment. But after the game, I agreed to have an X-ray taken in order to calm the fears of our team physician.

I was told that I had a torn Achilles tendon, an injury that has ended the playing careers of professional athletes. An article soon came out in our newspaper that said I was out for the season, and, not only that, I'd be unlikely ever to play football again. I considered the newspaper's prediction like a sentence given by a judge in a court of law, and it was a sentence I did not want to accept.

A passage from the Christian Science textbook, *Science and Health with Key to the Scriptures,* explains the basis for my mental protest at the time, "It is man's moral right to annul an unjust sentence, a sentence never inflicted by divine authority" (p. 381).

I decided to call a Christian Science practitioner for help. She agreed to pray for me, and she asked me to read and study ideas from the chapter, "Christian Science Practice" in *Science and Health*—specifically page 393, lines 4–24. This section explains that because man (each one of us) reflects God, we each have the ability and right to reject the pain and suffering that result from a matter-based view of reality. To me, this meant that if I learned to acknowledge God as the only power, I could expect my body to reflect God's perfection.

At first, progress toward healing seemed slow, and after a week of consistent prayer with the practitioner, I told her I was concerned. That's when she pointed out that my feelings toward the player who had injured me were an important part of healing. Harboring feelings of hatred, revenge, and victimization would only keep me from moving forward and having a complete healing.

In this case, I really needed to identify my opponent as a fellow child of God rather than as my enemy. Jesus forgave the people who put him on the cross. So I focused on expressing this Christ-like forgiveness, rather than indulging in thoughts of unfairness and mistreatment.

I prayed to see how I reflected the synonyms of God found in *Science and Health*, "Principle; Mind; Soul; Spirit; Life; Truth; Love" (587:5). For example, I would declare that because God is Life, I must reflect and express all the qualities of Life, including freedom, balance, and unencumbered action. And my true spiritual self could never be injured or limited.

Less than a month after that first game, I was cleared to play by the team physician and rejoined my teammates. The team physician, an outspoken Christian, believed that my choice to turn to God in prayer had resulted in this "miracle" of healing. I finished the season, playing in the final four games with complete freedom.

Doug Moser
Vernon Hills, Illinois, USA

LEARN *more* HERE

These pages give extra information about the stories in this book. They are divided into sections telling about some of the People, Places, **Customs**, and **Concepts** that will help you understand Bible times and Jesus' teachings. There's also a Glossary section, which is like a dictionary. It explains words you might not know and tells about familiar words (like "bed") that meant something different during Bible times than they do today.

When you see a word in a story printed in a color, you can find that word in the section here that matches the word's color. Have fun using these sections to learn more about what life was like for Jesus and his followers.

CONCEPTS
CUSTOMS
GLOSSARY
PEOPLE
PLACES

CONCEPTS

Ascended/Ascension

The word "ascend" means "to rise up" or "to go from a lower to a higher level." When Jesus ascended, his thoughts didn't rise just a little higher spiritually. They rose as high as possible—above all thought of life as material. He rose to the point of completely understanding life as spiritual, so there was no material evidence of him left. That's why the disciples, who were more material in their thinking, couldn't see him anymore. (See Mark 16:19; Luke 24:51; Acts 1:9.)

Baptism

Typically, baptism means being washed or dipped in water as a sign of purification or renewal. The Bible first mentions the word "baptism" in the Gospels, where John the Baptist baptizes people with water as a way of showing that they are committing themselves to God. John explains, though, that Jesus will baptize in a more spiritual way (see Matthew 3:1–2, 11; Luke 3:15–16).

To Jesus, baptism meant being filled with the **Holy Spirit**—with the understanding of God's all-powerful, spiritual laws. After his resurrection, Jesus promised his followers that they would be baptized, or filled, with the Holy Spirit (see Acts 1:5, 8). And on the day of **Pentecost**, that's exactly what happened (see Acts 2:1–18).

Despite this, many of Jesus' followers in the early Christian church continued to baptize with water. This ritual showed that the people being baptized believed Jesus was the **Christ** and that they wanted to be his followers.

Many also understood that being baptized with water was a symbol of cleansing or purifying one's thinking. This is what Paul called "putting off the old man," getting rid of the belief that people are material, and "putting on the new man," lifting thought to see everyone's spiritual nature created by God (Colossians 3:9–10). With this spiritual understanding of the "new man," Jesus and his followers were able to heal sickness and sin and to overcome death.

Christ

The Greek word for "Christ" and the Hebrew word for "Messiah" mean "anointed" and refer to someone chosen to save people from all kinds of troubles—from sickness, sin, and even death. Many Jews believed the Messiah would be a special king who would deliver them from their enemies.

Jesus didn't think of himself as a king. He saw himself fulfilling his spiritual mission to heal and teach—and to show people the "**kingdom of God**" on earth (see Luke 4:17–21). He saw the Christ as his—and everyone's—perfect, spiritual nature. And he understood that this nature comes from God. Jesus knew that God creates only good, so he saw problems—sickness, sin, and death—as "enemies" of God. Jesus wasn't afraid of these enemies because he knew they had no real place or power since God, good, is All and all-powerful. This truth destroyed the "enemies," or problems that people had, by healing the people. In this way, Jesus revealed God's goodness, God's kingdom, right where the problems seemed to be.

Because of the many wonderful healings resulting from Jesus' understanding of the Christ, people began calling him "Christ Jesus."

Demon(s)

In Jesus' time, people believed that invisible beings were everywhere—in the water, the air, the desert, the fields, the night, and even inside people. These beings were called by many different names: demons, devils, evil spirits, or unclean spirits. People believed these beings caused diseases, unhappiness, and many other problems, and magicians came up with rules for getting rid of them. People thought the rules worked, but they also believed the beings could come back. Most people thought these beings worked for the Devil or Satan (a power opposed to God). They also thought that people who had these beings inside them were "unclean" or impure. (See also **Laws of Cleanness**.)

Faith

In 13 of Jesus' healings, he says "faith" or "believing" is important. The Greek word for "faith" means "conviction" or "belief." To have conviction means "to be firm." Jesus told his disciples to "have faith in God" and not to doubt (Mark 11:22–23). When he asked people to have faith or to believe, Jesus wanted them to be firm in their understanding that he healed by the power of God. He also said that anyone who had strong faith could heal through God's power (see Mark 16:17–18).

Many people who were healed by Jesus had faith in him as the "Messiah" or "**Christ**." They sometimes called him the "Son of David" or "Son of God," both of which are names for the "Messiah" or "Christ." These terms refer to Jesus' spiritual nature—the presence of God, Spirit, in thought. This spiritual nature, or Christ-nature, heals because it is backed by the power of God. Jesus proved this over and over

again by healing sickness, sin, and death. In fact, people started calling him "Christ Jesus" because he expressed the Christ, God's spiritual nature, so fully. The more the disciples learned from Jesus, the better they got at expressing the Christ and healing through God's power, too.

When people who were healed by Jesus or his disciples said they believed in Christ Jesus, they were saying they understood that Jesus healed through the power of God. By having faith in Christ Jesus and his teachings and healings, people were welcoming God's power into their lives. This faith helped people see that they could also overcome sickness, sin, and death by following Christ Jesus' example.

Healed of Sins

Several times in the Bible, Jesus tells people they are healed of their sins, or he says, "Your sins are forgiven." The term "forgiven" means "wiped away," "cast away," "removed," "healed."

In Bible times, the Jews believed sin created a barrier or wall between sinners and God, keeping them from feeling God's love or help. They also thought that sin caused people to be sick.

The Jews believed that to have sins forgiven, people had to go through rituals required by Jewish law (see **Purification Rituals**). But Jesus had a different idea about how to heal sin. When he said people's sins were healed or forgiven, he was seeing what was really true about them as God's children. He was helping them see themselves as completely good. This freed them to do what was right. And when their thinking and actions were healed, their bodies were healed, too.

Holy Spirit

The Holy Spirit (also called the "Holy Ghost") refers to the Spirit of God that is always present. Many great leaders and prophets in the Bible were filled with the Spirit of God—with thoughts of God's power and goodness. But Jesus had an even higher understanding of the Spirit of God. He knew that God, who is Spirit, is the *only* power, so God's laws are all-powerful. Jesus also knew that we are created in God's image and likeness—spiritual and perfect—and that God governs us with all-good and all-powerful laws. The Holy Spirit heals sickness and sin and restores life. Through his healing and teaching, Jesus encouraged people to see themselves and others as God's children and to rely on God's laws of good for all their needs.

Kingdom of God

Jews thought that the **Messiah** would bring the kingdom of God. They often imagined this kingdom as a great feast celebrating victory over enemies. Jews, who called themselves the "children of the kingdom," believed that they would sit at this feast with the Messiah, along with their ancestors Abraham, Isaac, and Jacob. They didn't think Gentiles would be included at the feast.

But Jesus told the Jews they couldn't join the feast just because they were Jews. They needed to have **faith** in order to get in. And Jesus added that Gentiles from many parts of the world, if they had faith, would also sit down at that feast. (The centurion who asked Jesus to heal his servant is a good example of the kind of Gentile who would have a seat at the feast because of his faith. See "Centurion's Servant Healed of Paralysis," p. 41.) Jesus even said that Jews who did not have faith would be cast out of the feast—the kingdom—into "outer darkness" and, therefore, would be disappointed, bitter, and

very angry (see Matthew 8:11–12). Jesus may have been helping the Jews see that those without faith in the power of God to heal would miss out on the joy of the kingdom of God, God's ever-present love and goodness.

Light of the World

Jesus said that he was sent by God to be the "light of the world" (John 8:12; John 9:5). This light was the spiritual truth Jesus knew and lived. He saw clearly what was true about everyone. He knew that God is all-good and all-powerful and makes everyone in the image and likeness of God, perfect and good. This truth that Jesus knew was and is like a light that destroys the darkness of sickness, sin, and death.

Messiah

The Hebrew word for "Messiah" and the Greek word for "Christ" mean "anointed" and refer to someone chosen to save people from all kinds of troubles—from sickness, sin, and even death. Many Jews believed the Messiah would be a special king who would deliver them from their enemies.

Jesus didn't think of himself as a king. He saw himself fulfilling his spiritual mission to heal and teach—and to show people the "**kingdom of God**" on earth (see Luke 4:17–21). He saw the Christ as his—and everyone's—perfect, spiritual nature. And he understood that this nature comes from God. Jesus knew that God creates only good, so he saw problems—sickness, sin, and death—as "enemies" of God. Jesus wasn't afraid of these enemies because he knew they had no real place or power since God, good, is All and all-powerful. This truth destroyed the "enemies," or problems that people had, by healing the people. In this way, Jesus revealed God's goodness, God's kingdom, right where the problems seemed to be.

Because of the many wonderful healings resulting from Jesus' understanding of the Christ, people began calling him "Christ Jesus."

Unclean Spirits

In Jesus' time, people believed that invisible beings were everywhere—in the water, the air, the desert, the fields, the night, and even inside people. These beings were called by many different names: demons, devils, evil spirits, or unclean spirits. People believed these beings caused diseases, unhappiness, and many other problems, and magicians came up with rules for getting rid of them. People thought the rules worked, but they also believed the beings could come back. Most people thought these beings worked for the Devil or Satan (a power opposed to God). They also thought that people who had these beings inside them were "unclean" or impure. (See also **Laws of Cleanness**.)

Word

To the Jews, God's word had power. When it was spoken, people expected to see something happen. The prophets before Jesus' time (see **Old Testament**), who spoke what they heard from God, said that the **Messiah** was coming to teach the power of God's word. And they were right. Jesus' teaching was the "gospel," or "good news," about God's powerful love for everyone.

In Greek, the language of the **New Testament**, "word" is *logos*. One of the meanings of *logos* is "something said, including the thought behind it." The Gospel of John gives a more spiritual meaning—it refers to the word as *being* God (see John 1:1). So, the word has all the power of God's thought behind it. When God's word is spoken, it is so powerful that it heals and restores life.

Jesus taught and proved that the power of the word—of good thoughts from God—could heal. That power could even heal people if they were far away (see "Nobleman's Son Healed of Illness," p. 36; "Centurion's Servant Healed of Paralysis," p. 41). And his disciples showed that Jesus' teaching, which helped them understand the word of God, was powerful, too. It made them able to heal the same way Jesus did. (You can read about the disciples healing people beginning on p. 180.)

CUSTOMS

"Don't tell anyone . . ."

Jesus told some of the people he healed not to tell anyone about their healings. Here are some possible reasons he said this:

- The people he healed were inspired and grateful. If they talked about being healed, the scribes and Pharisees might ask them questions they didn't know how to answer, and that might make them doubt what they had experienced with Jesus. Perhaps Jesus was protecting them. He didn't want them to lose their **faith** and inspiration.

- Lots of talk about being healed by Jesus might cause people to come to him just to see something exciting happen. And these people might crowd out the ones who actually wanted to learn about God.

- If crowds gathered around Jesus, the Jewish religious leaders might become jealous and try to get rid of him.

- Crowds might start calling Jesus "Messiah," thinking that he was the king they were expecting to save them. Jesus didn't want people to think he was a king. He needed time to teach them and show them by healing and raising the dead that the **Messiah** is God's spiritual nature, or Christ, which belonged not just to him but to everyone. He wanted them to see that he healed through the Christ and that they could, too.

Feast of Passover

This is an eight-day **festival** held each year to remember how God saved the Jews from slavery in Egypt.

Feast of Tabernacles

This was one of three big **festivals** held in Jerusalem and still celebrated today throughout the Jewish community. Traditionally, people built simple shelters out of branches and vines and slept and ate in them during this festival. Doing this reminded them of an earlier time when, after escaping slavery in Egypt, the Jews had wandered in the wilderness for 40 years, living in tents.

Water and light are important symbols at this festival, which lasts seven days. In Jesus' time, the priests participated in the ritual of gathering water from the **Pool of Siloam** each day and bringing it to the **Temple** altar for a gratitude offering. At night, the Temple area was lighted with huge menorahs (oil lamp stands).

Festival(s)

Jewish law provides for special religious celebrations each year called "feasts" or "festivals." In Jesus' day, these three festivals were so important that the law required every Jewish male, beginning at age 13, to go to the **Temple** in Jerusalem to celebrate:

- **Feast of Passover**
- Feast of **Pentecost**
- **Feast of Tabernacles**

Like other Jews, Jesus celebrated these feasts at the Temple in Jerusalem.

Healing by Touch

In Bible times, many people believed they could be healed if they touched, or were touched by, someone who was very holy or close to God. But Jesus understood that people were not healed by physical contact. He knew that God healed them and that it was his clear understanding of God's power that enabled him to bring healing to people.

In half of Jesus' 30 recorded healings, there is no mention of him touching the person. And in three of these cases, he healed people he couldn't touch because they were not there with him. Many times when Jesus did touch people, he made it clear that their **faith** had healed them, not his touch.

For Jesus' apostles' healings, only half mention that people were touched in some way. Of those, two were just helped to their feet.

Even though touching and being touched don't heal, they have interesting meanings in the Bible:

- **Being touched ("laying on of hands"):** The act of "laying on of hands" was a symbol of God's power to heal. Sometimes Jesus and his apostles touched people to express love. This helped people feel cared for and removed their fear. Once they were no longer afraid, people were more receptive to the healing power of God.

- **Touching the holy person or his clothing:** Many people believed that if they touched a holy person, his shadow, or his clothing, they would be healed. The bodies and clothes of Jesus and his apostles had no special power to heal, but the faith people had in their ability to heal was powerful.

Jesus' thinking was so spiritual that he could tell when people needed healing without speaking to them or seeing them. Even if he could not see or feel a person touching him, Jesus felt the presence and power of God when that person was healed.

Jewish Customs—Burial

After washing the body of the person who had died, people wrapped it in long strips of cloth. If they could afford spices, they spread them on the cloth. People thought that using a lot of spices showed how much the person was loved. (Jesus' wealthy friends used 75 pounds of spices when they prepared his body for burial!) Jews believed the body should be buried within 24 hours of the death.

The bodies of wealthy people were often placed in tombs—either caves or places carved out of big rocks. The entrance to a tomb was usually sealed with a large, wheel-shaped rock. People who didn't have a lot of money wrapped the bodies of their dead in cloth and buried them in the ground instead of in tombs. (See also **Jewish Customs—Mourning**.)

Jewish Customs—Guests

A Jewish host often welcomed guests to his home and showed friendship and respect in these ways:

- Because many parts of Palestine were hot and dusty much of the year, the host provided water for guests to wash their feet. Sometimes a servant washed the guest's feet.

- The host greeted the guest with a kiss on the cheek, sometimes on both cheeks.

• To honor the guest, the host poured a few drops of olive oil on the guest's head. (Oil was a symbol of gladness.) To show even more respect, the host used perfumed oil, which was more expensive.

Jewish Customs—Mourning

In Bible times, when someone died, people visited the person's family to show their love and to help them. The usual mourning period for family members was seven days.

Jews also followed certain rituals to show their grief. People who were mourning wore clothes made of sackcloth—a rough, dark-colored material made of goat's or camel's hair. Often they "rent," or tore, their clothes. Some put ashes or dust on their heads.

Immediately after a person died, the family hired "mourners" (usually women) to weep and wail—to cry out very loudly and sing sad songs. They also hired people to play musical instruments, most often flutes. For example, the Jewish expectation was that even the poorest man must provide at least two flutes and one wailing woman for his wife's funeral.

Laws of Cleanness

The Jews believed they needed to obey certain laws in order for God to see them as "clean" or pure. They thought that the sick, the sinning, the dead, people who were not Jewish (see Gentiles), lepers, people with mental illnesses, and certain animals such as swine were "unclean" or impure. Jews believed that if they touched or were touched by someone or something unclean, they became unclean, too. To be clean or pure again, the unclean had to take part in special **purification rituals**.

Laws of Cleanness—Death

The Jews believed that the dead were "unclean" or impure. Jewish laws said that anyone who touched a dead body or a bed with a dead body on it was considered "unclean" or impure. The laws also said that anyone who entered the house where there was a dead body would be unclean. The unclean person was supposed to follow certain **purification rituals** to become clean or pure again. When Jesus touched the young man's bed in Nain, and when he entered Jairus' house and took Jairus' daughter by the hand, he was considered unclean (see "Widow's Son Brought Back to Life," p. 45, and "Jairus' Daughter Brought Back to Life," p. 69). But Jesus didn't let the Jewish laws stop him from helping others. He understood that God makes everyone perfect and spiritual and keeps them that way. And he knew that healing through God's power couldn't make him unclean or impure.

Laws of Cleanness—Sin

The Jews believed that sinners were "unclean" or impure and that anyone touched by a sinner would also be unclean or impure. A good Jew, and especially a prophet, was supposed to stay pure and holy. So people were surprised that Jesus was kind to sinners and didn't mind touching or being touched by them. (See "Woman Healed of Sin," p. 50.) Jesus saw these people as perfect children of God, not as sinners. That's why he was happy to be around them.

Pentecost

The word "Pentecost" in Greek means "fiftieth day." The Jews praised God for their grain harvest with a special Pentecost **festival** on the day after the seven-week harvest, the fiftieth day. (Seven weeks is 49 days: 7×7=49. The day after that is the fiftieth day: 49+1=50.)

Christians see the Pentecost described in the book of Acts as the day Jesus' followers were first filled with the **Holy Spirit** (see Acts 2:1–18). The Bible says that this Pentecost experience—being filled with the Holy Spirit—occurs for all of Jesus' followers, including those who follow his teachings today (see Acts 2:38–39).

Purification Rituals

According to Jewish laws, people considered "unclean" or impure had to follow certain rituals to become "clean" or pure again. For instance, after lepers were healed (see **Leprosy**), they couldn't return home until they had done what the priests told them to do. Often, they were told to make offerings, shave their bodies, and wash themselves many times. After the lepers had done these things, their families and friends believed they were healthy and "clean" or pure. (See also **Laws of Cleanness**.)

Sabbath Law(s)

"Sabbath" in Hebrew means "rest." Genesis, the first book in the Bible, says that God "rested on the seventh day" (Genesis 2:2). The Jews call the seventh day the "Sabbath." This is the day God knew creation was complete, and God blessed this day (see Genesis 2:3). The Fourth Commandment refers to this blessing: "Remember the sabbath day, to keep it holy" (Exodus 20:8).

The Jewish people believed that the way to keep the Sabbath holy was not to work. Their laws listed many things that should not be done on the Sabbath, including healing. But Jesus understood God's "Sabbath rest" in a deeper way. He knew that everything God creates is good and that God keeps this creation pure and perfect. So, Jesus "rested" as God did—by seeing the holiness of God's perfect, spiritual creation. That kind of seeing heals—every day. Jesus knew that healing by seeing God's all-good creation is the best way to keep the Sabbath holy.

Spit

In Jesus' time, spit had at least two symbolic meanings:

- **Healing:** People thought of spit as a cure for small wounds, so spit became a symbol of healing. But Jesus knew that spit had no power to heal. And no one would have thought that touching parts of the head with spit could heal deafness, speech problems, or blindness. In one of his healings, Jesus may have used spit in a different way—to help people understand that he was going to heal them (see "Man Healed of Blindness from Birth," p. 134). (See also **Healing by Touch**.)

- **Disgust:** Spitting could also show that something or someone was worthless. When Jesus spit, he was rejecting the lie that anything material has power. Jesus knew that all power comes from God, and this understanding brought healing.

GLOSSARY

Bed

There were various types of beds in Bible times. Some were simple floor mats, possibly made of straw. Others had wooden frames and short legs and were often decorated beautifully. Some beds were like stretchers. They were made of fabric or woven straw with wooden poles attached, which made it easy to carry someone who was sick or couldn't walk.

Blasphemy

In the Bible, "blasphemy" means "something that dishonors God." It was a serious wrong that could lead to severe punishment or even death. The Bible tells of many times when the scribes and Pharisees accused Jesus of blasphemy. For example, they thought it was blasphemy when Jesus said he could forgive or heal sins. They believed only God could forgive sins, so when Jesus claimed he could do what God does, they thought he was making himself equal to God. They also accused Jesus of blasphemy when he called himself the "Son of God" and when he said, "I and my Father are one" (John 10:30).

Church(es)

The Greek word for "church" means "gathering." Early Christians had no church buildings. A church was a group of followers. These groups met either outdoors or in someone's home.

Leprosy

In the Bible, the word "leprosy" is used to refer to a variety of skin diseases. If people had a skin disease, they had to go to one of the Jewish priests, who would tell them what kind of skin disease it was. If it was serious, the priest called it "leprosy," and the person, who was called a "leper," was said to be "unclean," meaning impure.

Lepers had to follow **laws of cleanness**. Because the Jews thought that touching or being touched by a leper would make them unclean too, lepers had to live outside town, away from anyone except other lepers. To make sure people knew to stay away from them, lepers had to yell out, "Unclean! Unclean!" They also were not allowed to go to the Temple in Jerusalem. Once a leper was healed, he had to go back to the priest to be declared "clean." (See also **Purification Rituals**.)

Lord

The term "Lord" is often used as another name for "God." Sometimes these terms are combined, and God is called "Lord God." But the term "Lord" doesn't always refer to God. It can also refer to a person who is in charge of others. When used this way, "Lord" is a sign of respect for the person's authority. Jesus was often called "Lord" out of respect for his understanding of God and God's laws—and for the way he taught and healed with power and authority.

Master

The Hebrew and Greek words that mean "master" or "teacher" were titles of respect. People called Jesus by these titles not because he had gone to a special school but because he taught about God and God's laws with great power and understanding.

New Testament

The New Testament, written in Greek, begins with Jesus' birth and tells about his life and his followers. The Gospels—the books of Matthew, Mark, Luke, and John—are the first four books of the New Testament. They tell about Jesus' many healings and about his crucifixion, resurrection, and **ascension**. They also include his

270

famous Sermon on the Mount and the story of his Last Supper with his disciples. In addition, the New Testament describes the apostles' healings and Paul's travels and teachings. It also contains many of Paul's letters to the early Christian churches. The last book of the New Testament is Revelation, which ends with a description of God's perfect, spiritual kingdom. Altogether, the last 27 books of the Bible make up the New Testament.

Old Testament

The Old Testament, written in Hebrew, explains the history of the Jews and tells about Jesus' life, long before he was born. It also describes important people who lived before Jesus' time, including Abraham, Daniel, David, Esther, Isaiah, Jacob, Job, Joseph, Moses, Naomi, Nehemiah, Noah, Ruth, Solomon, and many others. The Old Testament is full of examples of God healing and protecting people—and talking directly to them. These examples include the stories about Noah's ark, Moses and the burning bush, the children of Israel crossing the Red Sea, David and Goliath, the three Hebrew captives in the fiery furnace, and Daniel in the lions' den. The beautiful poems in Psalms are part of the Old Testament, too. Altogether, the first 39 books of the Bible make up the Old Testament.

Paralyzed

If someone is paralyzed, he or she can't move some part of the body and doesn't have feeling there. The Bible uses the word "palsy" to describe this problem.

Peace

The word "peace" is used throughout the Bible. The Hebrew word for "peace" is *shalom*. It has many different meanings: prosperity, well-being, wholeness, health, security, harmony, happiness, quietness, calmness, rest, being at one with God.

Sabbath

"Sabbath" in Hebrew means "rest." Genesis, the first book in the Bible, says that God "rested on the seventh day" (Genesis 2:2). The Jews call the seventh day the "Sabbath." This is the day God knew creation was complete, and God blessed this day (see Genesis 2:3). The Fourth Commandment refers to this blessing: "Remember the sabbath day, to keep it holy" (Exodus 20:8).

Each week, Sabbath services were held in synagogues. These services consisted of prayer, singing psalms, reading from the scriptures, and teaching. The man in charge, the "ruler," chose men to read and teach. Jesus was chosen many times to teach in synagogues. Jews still hold Sabbath services in synagogues around the world today.

Teacher

The Hebrew and Greek words that mean "teacher" or "master" were titles of respect. People called Jesus by these titles not because he had gone to a special school but because he taught about God and God's laws with great power and understanding.

PEOPLE

Ananias

The Bible says that Ananias was a "disciple," but he was not one of Jesus' twelve closest disciples. He was a follower of Jesus who probably left Jerusalem and settled in Damascus because Jesus' followers were being persecuted in Jerusalem after Stephen's death. Ananias had a vision of **Christ** Jesus telling him to go and heal Saul, who was one of the followers' worst persecutors. Ananias had many doubts and fears about going to Saul, but he obeyed. As soon as he saw Saul, Ananias healed him of blindness and welcomed him as a new follower.

Apostle(s)

The word "apostle" means "one sent out." Three of the Gospels tell about the disciples being sent out to teach and heal (see Matthew 10:1–8; Mark 6:7–13; Luke 10:1–9, 17–19). Jesus' closest disciples included Simon Peter, Andrew, James (the son of Zebedee), John, Philip, Bartholomew, Thomas, Matthew, James (the son of Alphaeus), and Simon (see Matthew 10:2–4). These men and others, like Paul, who went out to heal and to teach and preach the good news about Jesus, were called "apostles."

Aristarchus

This follower from Thessalonica traveled with Paul to help him share Jesus' teachings. A loyal friend, Aristarchus even traveled with Paul to Rome when he was taken there as a prisoner. Aristarchus probably stayed with Paul for as long as Paul lived.

Barnabas

This kind and generous follower helped share Jesus' teachings, sometimes traveling with Paul. Barnabas also traveled with John Mark to teach in Cyprus, the island where Barnabas grew up. (See also p. 289.)

Centurion

A centurion was a soldier in the Roman army. The Romans ruled a large area, including **Palestine**. Their army was divided into legions (about six thousand men), which were divided into smaller and smaller groups called cohorts, maniples, and centuries. A centurion commanded a century of 50–100 soldiers. (See also **Roman Empire**.)

Christian(s)

After Jesus **ascended**, his disciples shared what they had learned from him about the **Christ**— God's perfect, spiritual nature. Jesus expressed the Christ so completely that he was called Christ Jesus, but he had taught the disciples that all of God's children express the Christ. As the disciples shared this good news and healed through the power of the Christ, more and more people believed in Jesus' teachings. These followers of Christ Jesus were the first people called Christians.

Daughter(s) of Abraham

In biblical times, as today, Jewish men and women called themselves the sons or daughters of Abraham. The Jewish people trace their history to a single individual named Abraham whose story is told in the book of Genesis (see chapters 12–25). Abraham is the first patriarch in the Hebrew Bible (see **Old Testament**). (The word "patriarch" means "father," and refers to the male head of a family or tribe. The wife of a patriarch or female head of a family is called a "matriarch.") When Jesus called a woman a "daughter of Abraham," he was reminding her and others around her that she was an important and valued member of the community.

Disciple(s)

The Greek word for "disciple" means "learner" or "student." In the **New Testament**, this word often refers to Jesus' twelve closest disciples—Simon Peter, Andrew, James (the son of Zebedee), John, Philip, Bartholomew, Thomas, Matthew, James (the son of Alphaeus), Lebbaeus, Simon, and Judas (see Matthew 10:2–4). But other followers were called disciples, too. For example, Tabitha was called a disciple (see Acts 9:36). A disciple can mean anyone—man, woman, or child—who studies and follows someone's teachings, no matter when that teacher lived. By studying and following Jesus' teachings, we can be his disciples today.

Follower(s)

Jesus' first followers heard him teach and saw him heal people—or were healed by him themselves. They followed him physically from place to place, listening to him and learning. After

Jesus' **ascension**, more people became followers of Jesus' teachings as they learned about them from his disciples and apostles—or were healed by them. In some cases, many people became followers all at once (see Acts 2:41; Acts 5:14). The followers played an important part in the growth of Christianity. They were the first people called "Christians."

Sometimes the Bible uses other terms to refer to the followers, including "believers," "disciples," and "brethren" or brothers and sisters (see, for example, Acts 5:14; Acts 6:1; Acts 6:3). And sometimes it uses the term "saints" (Acts 9:13), which means those who are "Godlike" or "pure."

Gentile(s)

The word "Gentile" means "Greek" in the **New Testament**. It refers to people whose customs, language, and religious practices were different from the Jews'. Gentiles worshiped many different gods, so the Jews separated themselves from them to keep their own worship of the one God pure. (See also **Laws of Cleanness**.)

Jew(s)

As a group of people, Jews, also known as Hebrews, trace their ancestry back to Abraham (originally named Abram). Abraham was called by God to leave his country, Ur in Mesopotamia, and to start a nation of people who would worship the one God. He obeyed, and traveled to Canaan, or **Palestine**, where God promised him many descendants and a place for them to live (see Genesis 12:1–7). Through several generations, God renewed this promise with Abraham's son Isaac and Isaac's son Jacob (see Genesis 26:1–5; Genesis 35:9–12). Jacob was also called

Jew(s) *(continued)*

Israel, so his descendants were often called the children of Israel, or Israelites.

During a long famine, Jacob's son Joseph (Abraham's great-grandson) encouraged his father and brothers and their families to move to Egypt. There was a famine in most of the area but not in Egypt, thanks to the planning and preparation Joseph had made while working for Pharaoh, the king of Egypt.

Over several generations, the children of Israel increased greatly in number, which worried the Egyptians. Afraid that they would be overpowered, the Egyptians enslaved them. Eventually, Moses led the children of Israel out of Egypt and began the long journey back to Canaan, the Promised Land where God had told Abraham his descendants would live. During this journey, Moses, who received the Ten Commandments from God, urged the people again and again to worship the one God.

The Israelites arrived in the Promised Land—the land of Israel. They lived there independently as twelve tribes. King David united them. He conquered a city called **Jerusalem** and made it his capital. Later his son King Solomon built the first **Temple** there. The kingdom divided after Solomon's reign. The northern kingdom was called Israel, whose capital was **Samaria**, and Jerusalem remained the capital of the southern kingdom, which was called Judah. Each kingdom had its own kings. After two hundred years, the northern kingdom was conquered, and its tribes have been called the ten "lost tribes of Israel."

The southern kingdom was conquered by the Babylonians in 587–586 BC. They destroyed the city and Temple, and sent the people of Judah to Babylon, where they lived in exile for several decades. Then King Cyrus of Persia allowed them to return to Judah and rebuild the Temple. At that point, they were known as Jews. Except for a brief period, they lived under other people's rule—first under the Persians, then the Greeks, and then the Romans. When Jesus was born, the Romans ruled over Israel. Because the Jews couldn't have their own rulers, their religious leaders—the **priests**, **scribes**, **Pharisees**, and Sadducees—became very important.

John

John was one of Jesus' closest **disciples** and may have been the youngest one. Many believe that he is the person referred to in the Bible as "that disciple whom Jesus loved" (John 21:7) and that he was the only one of Jesus' twelve **apostles** at his crucifixion. After Jesus' resurrection and **ascension**, John was a leader of the **followers** in **Jerusalem**. Later, he traveled to teach and preach in **Samaria**. (See also p. 289.)

John Mark

John Mark, or Marcus, traveled with **Paul** and **Barnabas** for a short time on their first missionary journey, but John Mark left before the trip was over. Barnabas wanted to take him on his next journey with Paul, but Paul refused. This disagreement caused Paul and Barnabas to separate. Barnabas went ahead and took John Mark with him to teach in Cyprus. Later, Paul spoke kindly of John Mark.

Luke

The Bible suggests that Luke was a traveling companion of **Paul**'s (see II Timothy 4:11), and most scholars believe that he was a **Gentile**. Colossians 4:14 calls him "the beloved physician." Scholars agree that the Gospel of Luke and the Book of Acts were written by the same person, but they don't know if it was Luke or someone else not named in the Bible. These two books make up a quarter of the New Testament and are the only ones in the Bible written by a Gentile.

Lydia

Lydia was a businesswoman and was probably wealthy. She sold expensive purple cloth—a color that many rich people loved. It's very possible that she was a Gentile who prayed with the Jewish women. Lydia was from the ancient Greek city of Thyatira, which is now part of Turkey. At the time she met Paul, she was living in Philippi, a Roman settlement across the Aegean Sea. She was probably in Philippi to expand her business selling cloth. She may have been the first person in what we call Europe today to become a follower of Jesus (see Acts 16:13–15).

Paul/Saul

This apostle was born in Tarsus, an important port for ships and the capital of Cilicia, a province in the Roman Empire. Though a Jew, he also had Roman citizenship. His Hebrew, or Jewish, name was Saul. His Roman name was Paul. For a long time, Saul persecuted Jesus' followers. Then, while on a trip to Damascus, he became blind and heard a voice that said it was Jesus speaking to him. Saul was led the rest of the way to Damascus, and a few days later, Ananias healed him of his blindness. Saul then became one of Jesus' followers. In fact, he went on to become a leader among Jesus' apostles. He healed himself and others and shared the good news about Jesus' life and teachings with many people, especially Gentiles. Paul wrote many of the letters in the New Testament. His own story is told in Acts. Altogether, about half the books in the New Testament are by or about Paul. (See also p. 290.)

Peter

This disciple was called by several different names: Simon, Peter, Simon Peter, and Cephas. Peter was a fisherman before he became Jesus' student. He was an eager learner, quick and enthusiastic in everything he did. He often spoke for the other disciples. Peter became a leader in the early Christian church. (See also p. 283.)

Pharisee(s)

The Pharisees were a group of Jewish religious leaders who loved to obey the Ten Commandments, the laws God gave Moses for the children of Israel to follow (see Exodus 20:3–4, 7–8, 12–17). But the Pharisees also obeyed hundreds of other oral and written laws. Many Jews looked up to the Pharisees. So the Pharisees began to feel that they were more obedient to God's commands than other people were. And they felt they needed to watch everyone else to make sure they were obeying all the Jewish laws. Over time, the Pharisees became so focused on Jewish laws that they sometimes overlooked the importance of the supreme laws, the Ten Commandments from God.

Jesus, on the other hand, loved the deep meaning of God's commandments. He taught about God's love, and he proved this love by healing. If following a Jewish law meant he couldn't be loving to people or heal them, Jesus didn't obey it. This upset the Pharisees. It also bothered them that big crowds were following Jesus instead of them. Eventually, some of the Pharisees got so angry at Jesus that they looked for ways to kill him.

Philip

Two people named Philip play important roles in the **New Testament**. One of Jesus' twelve **disciples** was named Philip. He was from **Bethsaida**. The Philip mentioned in this book is Philip the evangelist, who was born in Caesarea. He was chosen by the **apostles**, along with **Stephen** and five others, to help care for the **followers** by serving tables (see Acts 6:1–5). As an evangelist, Philip preached the gospel—the good news about Jesus' life and teachings. He also healed through God's power. Philip started this holy work in **Jerusalem** but later traveled to **Samaria** to preach and heal there as well. (See also p. 289.)

Priest(s)

The priests were important religious leaders. They took turns working at the **Temple** in **Jerusalem**. On certain occasions, they said special prayers or blessings, blew large trumpets, and blew the shofar (a trumpet made from a ram's horn). They also performed rituals that the **Jews** believed would make people "clean" or pure. (See also **Purification Rituals**.)

Prophet(s)

Prophets appear throughout the Bible. Their love for God was so strong and pure that they were wide awake to God's **word**—the spiritual truths God was showing and telling them. Prophets challenged people to obey God's word. They spoke the truth even to kings! Deborah inspired the Israelites in battle. Moses, Elijah, and Elisha showed the power of God's word by healing many different kinds of sickness. Elijah and Elisha even brought people back to life. They saw God as all-powerful, and this spiritual seeing led to wonderful healings.

Long before Jesus' time, Moses told of a great prophet who would come someday (see Deuteronomy 18:15). Isaiah described this prophet as someone filled with the Spirit of God who would preach good news to the poor, heal the brokenhearted (those who are very sad), deliver the captives (those who can't break free from evil), and give sight to the blind. Jesus read Isaiah's words in the Nazareth **synagogue** one **Sabbath** and told the people that he was that prophet (see Isaiah 61:1–2; Luke 4:16–21).

Samaritan(s)

The Samaritans had the same ancestors as the **Jews**, but over time they married **Gentiles**, so the Jews looked down on them. The Jews and Samaritans also had many long-standing religious disagreements. For example, the Samaritans accepted only the first five books of the Bible as sacred (the books called the "Torah," or "law"), while the Jews thought of the entire Hebrew Bible as holy (see **Old Testament**). The Samaritans also differed from the Jews in their interpretation of the laws, and they disagreed about where to build the **Temple**. The Jews built theirs in **Jerusalem**, while the Samaritans built their temple in Gerizim.

These differences didn't stop Jesus from loving the Samaritans and healing them (see "Ten Men Healed of Leprosy," p. 124). And he encouraged his **followers** to treat Samaritans the same way they would want to be treated—with kindness and love (see Luke 9:52–56; Luke 10:30–37; Luke 17:11–19; John 4:3–42).

Sanhedrin

The Sanhedrin was the highest Jewish governing group during Jesus' time. The members of the Sanhedrin met in **Jerusalem**. The group's leader was called the "high **priest**."

Saul/Paul

This apostle was born in Tarsus, an important port for ships and the capital of Cilicia, a province in the Roman Empire. Though a Jew, he also had Roman citizenship. His Hebrew, or Jewish, name was Saul. His Roman name was Paul. For a long time, Saul persecuted Jesus' followers. Then, while on a trip to Damascus, he became blind and heard a voice that said it was Jesus speaking to him. Saul was led the rest of the way to Damascus, and a few days later, Ananias healed him of his blindness. Saul then became one of Jesus' followers. In fact, he went on to become a leader among Jesus' apostles. He healed himself and others and shared the good news about Jesus' life and teachings with many people, especially Gentiles. Paul wrote many of the letters in the New Testament. His own story is told in Acts. Altogether, about half the books in the New Testament are by or about Paul. (See also p. 290.)

Scribes

Scribes studied the Torah (the first five books of the Bible, which include the Ten Commandments) and copied them onto scrolls from other scrolls. They also studied many other oral and written laws and taught what these laws meant and how people should obey them. But their teaching didn't have the spiritual power of Jesus' teaching because they focused on the words instead of their deeper meaning. Jesus taught with complete confidence in the power of God's word, which heals.

Silas

Paul chose Silas, also called Silvanus, to travel with him to Macedonia. While there, in the city of Philippi, some of the people who didn't like what they were teaching about God beat them up and put them in prison. But as they prayed, they were freed (see Acts 16:23–26).

Silas helped Paul write some of his letters (see I and II Thessalonians). He also helped Paul as he preached and healed in several cities in the area, including Corinth. When Paul left Corinth, Silas stayed there teaching the people about God.

Son(s) of Abraham

In biblical times, as today, Jewish men and women called themselves the sons or daughters of Abraham. The Jewish people trace their history to a single individual named Abraham whose story is told in the book of Genesis (see chapters 12–25). Abraham is the first patriarch in the Hebrew Bible (see Old Testament). (The word "patriarch" means "father," and refers to the male head of a family or tribe. The wife of a patriarch or female head of a family is called a "matriarch.") When Jesus called a man a "son of Abraham," he was reminding the man and others around him that he was an important and valued member of the community.

Son of David

In the Old Testament, this term refers to David's sons or to those men who trace their ancestry back to David. Jesus was in this latter group, but that was not what people meant when they used it to refer to him. In the New Testament, when people called Jesus the "Son of David," they were referring to him as the Messiah, Christ, or Son of God. They saw his spiritual understanding and power, which they hoped could help them—and it did (see "Two Men Healed of Blindness," p. 81; "Woman's Daughter Healed of Illness," p. 94; "Bartimaeus Healed of Blindness," p. 151).

Son of God/Son of Man

Jesus most often referred to himself as the "Son of man." Others usually referred to him as the "Son of God." The fact that Jesus was called both "Son of man" and "Son of God" helps us see that, although he was human, his spirituality enabled him to heal. Both today and in Jesus' time, this helped people understand that their spiritual nature as sons and daughters of God—expressing complete faith in God's love and all-power—gave them power to heal, too. Jesus wanted them to know that they could heal the same way he did. (Other names for the Son of God are "Messiah," "Christ," and "Son of David.")

Stephen

Stephen helped take care of Jesus' followers. He also healed people and shared Jesus' teachings (see Acts 6:8). Even when he was being stoned to death by those who disliked what he taught, he stayed true to Jesus' teachings by showing love toward his enemies (see Acts 7:59–60). (See also p. 291.)

Tabitha

The Bible says this woman was a "disciple," meaning "student." In fact, Tabitha is the only woman in the Bible specifically called a disciple of Jesus. She was full of "almsdeeds," which means she was always caring for poor and needy people, giving them gifts and helping them. Tabitha did many "good works," or acts of love and kindness. The other followers loved and respected her a great deal. Her Hebrew name is "Tabitha," and her Greek name is "Dorcas." In both languages, the name means "gazelle," which is a small antelope. The author of Acts may have used both her Hebrew and Greek names because some people understood Greek better than Hebrew, and he wanted all of them to know that she expressed grace and gentleness—like a gazelle.

Timothy

Timothy, or Timotheus, was from Lystra. Paul loved him like a son. At times Timothy traveled with Paul, and at other times Paul sent him to different places, such as Thessalonica, to teach and help the followers there. Later, Paul put him in charge of the church in Ephesus.

Woman/Women

Though women aren't mentioned in the Bible as often as men, they were very important in the growth of Christianity. In Bible times, women did not have the same rights as men. They usually lived with their father, husband, or son, had children, and managed the household. But some had special roles. For example, Jesus' mother Mary listened very closely to God and brought the baby Jesus into the world. Anna, a prophetess (or female prophet), saw the baby and praised God. She told everyone who was waiting for the Messiah about the baby (see Luke 2:36–38). Some women, like Mary Magdalene and Lydia, were independent and wealthy enough to help support Jesus and Paul in their missions (see Luke 8:2–3; Acts 16:14–15). There were many others such as Priscilla, who was a very active worker (see Acts 18:26), and Phebe, who was a deacon (see Romans 16:1).

Jesus treated women in a different way than most men did. He treated them as equal to men. He spoke to women in the streets and synagogues. He taught women. He healed women. He included them in his parables. Women traveled with him and became his followers. Two of his closest friends were Mary and Martha. Jesus helped both men and women discover their freedom, equality, and God-given goodness.

PLACES

Antioch (see Map 2)

Two cities with this name are mentioned in the New Testament, Antioch of Pisidia and Antioch in the Roman province of Syria. (Both cities are located in what is now Turkey.) Paul preached and taught in both cities, but usually when Antioch is mentioned in the Bible, it refers to Antioch in Syria. This ancient city—founded in 300 BC—was at the center of several trading routes. After the Romans conquered the Greeks, Antioch became one of the largest cities in the Roman Empire. Antioch in Syria is the first place where Jesus' followers were called "Christians" (see Acts 11:26).

Bethlehem (see Map 1)

Jesus was born in this small town about five miles south of Jerusalem. The word "Bethlehem" means "house of bread."

Bethsaida (see Map 1)

Bethsaida was the hometown of Peter, Andrew, and Philip (the disciple)—and possibly more of the disciples. It is located in a region called Gaulanitis, on the east side of the Sea of Galilee.

Capernaum (see Map 1)

Jesus began his ministry in Capernaum, a small city in Galilee, on the coast of the Sea of Galilee. People with products of all kinds traveled through Capernaum to the Mediterranean Sea and to Damascus. During Jesus' time, Roman soldiers were stationed in Capernaum. Many people there, including some of Jesus' disciples, earned their living as fishermen on the Sea of Galilee.

Caves

Caves were sometimes used as tombs or burial places. People believed that demons lived in dark places like caves.

City Gate

In Bible times, walls were built around cities to protect them from enemies. People's homes were inside these walls. The walls were made of stone and were very thick. Usually, the only way to get in and out of the city was through the gate, which was made of thick, strong wood.

Damascus (see Maps 1 and 2)

This was an important city in Syria and is one of the oldest cities in the world. In Bible times, it was about a six-day trip from Jerusalem.

Decapolis (see Map 1)

This was the region east of Samaria and Galilee. It was named "Decapolis" because ten cities in the area formed a group to help each other with trade and safety. The word "Decapolis" is made from two Greek words: *deca*, meaning "ten," and *polis*, meaning "city."

Galilee (see Map 1)

This was the region in the north of Palestine where Jesus grew up and spent most of his healing ministry. Almost all the disciples came from Galilee.

Iconium (see Map 2)

This city, located on a large, flat plain, was surrounded by rich, healthy soil that made excellent farmland. The area is part of Turkey today.

Jericho (see Map 1)

This was a busy city in the **Jordan River** valley about 15 miles northeast of **Jerusalem** and is one of the oldest cities in the world. It was located on a trade route and had a tax collector's office for collecting money from merchants using the route. Jericho was 825 feet below sea level, so in Jesus' parable about the good **Samaritan** (see Luke 10:30–37), when he spoke of a man going "down from Jerusalem to Jericho," it was literally true that the man traveled *down* to Jericho.

Jerusalem (see Maps 1 and 2)

Jerusalem was the most important city in Bible times. It is in the center of the region of **Palestine**, up in the hills of **Judea**. David captured Jerusalem and made it the capital of his kingdom and the center of worship. Solomon built the first **Temple** there. For centuries **Jews** traveled to Jerusalem for **festivals** held in the Temple. Jerusalem has had a long history of rulers and kings, war and peace, destruction and rebuilding. In Jesus' time, the Romans ruled Jerusalem and all of **Palestine**.

Jordan River (see Map 1)

The Jordan River flows from Mount Hermon in the north into a lake called the Sea of Galilee. From there, it continues down through the Jordan Valley until it reaches the Dead Sea, which is the lowest spot on earth, 1,300 feet below sea level.

The Jordan is an important river in the Bible and is mentioned often. Elisha directed Naaman to wash in the Jordan in order to be healed of **leprosy** (see II Kings 5:9–14). And John the Baptist preached by the Jordan and baptized Jesus there (see Matthew 3:13–17; Mark 1:9–11; Luke 3:21–22; see also **Baptism**).

Judea (see Map 1)

This is the Greek name for Judah. Judah, **Galilee**, and **Samaria** formed western **Palestine**. **Jerusalem**, where many of Jesus' healings took place, and **Bethlehem**, where he was born, were both in Judea.

Mount of Olives

From this large hill on the east side of **Jerusalem**, one could see every road to the city. When people like Jesus visited Jerusalem and couldn't find a place to spend the night in the city, they stayed on the Mount, where olive trees grew abundantly. Jesus often prayed there. One area of the Mount was a garden called Gethsemane (the Hebrew word for "oil press"), where olives were processed to make olive oil. Three of the Gospels tell about Jesus praying in the Mount of Olives before he was arrested and crucified. (See Matthew 26:36–46; Mark 14:32–42; Luke 22:39–47).

Palestine (see Map 2)

This term is used to describe a territory, on the eastern coast of the Mediterranean Sea, that is roughly equivalent to modern-day Israel. The area covered a number of regions, including **Samaria**, **Judea**, Idumea, **Galilee**, and parts of **Phoenicia** and **Decapolis**. In Jesus' time, Palestine was part of the **Roman Empire**.

Perea (see Map 1)

Perea was the land to the east of the **Jordan River** where John the Baptist preached. When traveling north and south, many **Jews** went through Perea to avoid **Samaria** on the west side of the river.

Phoenicia (see Map 2)

This was the region north of **Palestine** on the coast of the Mediterranean Sea. In the Bible, the word is spelled "Phenice" or "Phenicia." Tyre and Sidon were important cities in this region. When the **Jews** conquered Canaan, many of the people there (called Canaanites) moved into Phoenicia to live among the Phoenicians. The two groups lived so closely together that people from Phoenicia were often called Canaanites. Both groups worshiped idols and had a long history as enemies of the Jews.

Pool of Siloam

Jerusalem was built on the top of a hill so that the people who lived there would be safe. But the city had no water. That meant an enemy could keep the people in the city locked behind the city walls until they got so thirsty that they would give up. So in 715 BC, King Hezekiah built a tunnel that carried water from a spring outside the city wall into a pool he had dug inside the city. The pool was called "Siloam," which means "sent," because fresh water was now secretly sent to Jerusalem from outside the city walls.

Roman Empire

During the time of the **New Testament**, the Roman Empire was very powerful. It controlled all the lands around the Mediterranean Sea and was ruled by an emperor. Throughout the empire, Romans made laws, collected taxes, built roads, and stationed soldiers to watch the people and prevent them from rebelling against the Roman government.

Samaria (see Map 1)

This was the region between **Galilee** and **Judea**. The people who lived in Samaria were called **Samaritans**. The **Jews** saw the Samaritans as outsiders, and the Jews and Samaritans had many long-standing religious disagreements. For example, the Samaritans accepted only the first five books of the Bible as sacred (the books called the "Torah," or "law"), while the Jews thought of the entire Hebrew Bible as holy (see **Old Testament**). The Samaritans also differed from the Jews in their interpretation of the laws, and they disagreed about where to build the **Temple**. The Jews built theirs in **Jerusalem**, while the Samaritans built their temple in Gerizim.

Synagogue(s)

The **Jews** met in the synagogue to worship God on their **Sabbath** day, which is Saturday. Inside the synagogue were benches along the walls, a raised platform, oil lamps, and a cabinet to hold the scriptures, which were written on scrolls. Men and women may have sat in separate places. The "chief seats" in the synagogue were reserved for elders and important visitors. Jesus once rebuked the **scribes** and **Pharisees** for sitting in these seats to show off their importance (see Matthew 23:5–7; Mark 12:38–39).

The Sabbath service consisted of prayers, singing psalms, reading from the scriptures, and teaching. The man in charge, the "ruler," chose men to read and teach. Jesus was chosen many times to teach in synagogues.

Temple

The Temple in **Jerusalem** was the center of the
Jews' religious worship. More than just a place
of prayer and public worship, the Temple symbolized the presence of God. It was planned by
King David almost a thousand years before Jesus
was born and was built by David's son Solomon,
when he became king. The Temple was very
large and beautiful, built by skilled workers
using the finest wood, stone, silver, and gold.
The Temple contained a room called the "Holy
of Holies," where the ark of the covenant was
kept. The ark was a chest that contained the
stone tablets on which Moses wrote the Ten
Commandments that God had given him, as well
as other important items. The ark had disappeared by Jesus' time.

Solomon's Temple was destroyed by an enemy in
586 BC, and the Second Temple was rebuilt and
finished in 515 BC. King Herod the Great began
to expand and rebuild the Temple in 20 BC. It
was finished in AD 64.

Jesus' parents took him to the Temple for a
special ritual when he was a baby, and every
year they traveled from Nazareth to the Temple
for **festivals**. When Jesus was twelve years old,
he stayed after the Passover festival to listen to
and question the teachers in the Temple (see
Luke 2:41–47). When he grew up, Jesus traveled
to Jerusalem for festivals at the Temple and
sometimes taught in the courtyards surrounding
it. Once or twice Jesus made people leave this
area when they did not treat it with respect (see
Matthew 21:12–13; Mark 11:15–17).

the
LIFE
and TIMES
OF JESUS

God has always existed and is everywhere. For thousands of years and all around the world, people have wanted to feel close to God. This book begins with Jesus and the special spiritual understanding he brought as the Son of God. It would take another book—or maybe many books— to explain how people got to know God before Jesus' time.

Jesus grew up in the Jewish faith, with a strong belief in only one God. But he lived at a time when it was difficult for Jews to practice their faith. This had been true for many years.

Long before Jesus' time, in the late 330s BC, the Greeks conquered Palestine, where the Jews were living. Then, in 63 BC, the Romans took over Palestine. Under both the Greeks and Romans, the Jews had very little political control over their lives, but for the most part, they were free to worship the one God. Even so, many Jews had trouble staying firm in their faith because they were surrounded by people who worshipped many gods.

To try to keep the people faithful, the Jewish religious leaders, especially the scribes and Pharisees, developed many everyday religious laws and practices to keep people focused on God. But these laws were so detailed and strict that many Jews paid more attention to following the laws correctly than to feeling close to God.

The Jews' Hope for a Messiah and Jesus' Arrival

For hundreds of years under Greek and Roman rulers, the Jews had hoped that a Messiah (also called the Christ) would come to free them. The Hebrew word for "Messiah" and the Greek word for "Christ" mean "anointed"—chosen and dedicated—to save or deliver. Many thought the Messiah would be a king related to David. Centuries earlier, David had conquered Jerusalem and united the children of Israel as their king. People hoped that, along with getting rid of their enemies, this king, often called the "Son of David," would set up a kingdom that would last forever. Others believed the Messiah would be a priest who would purify the way the Jews worshiped God. Another group thought the Messiah would be a prophet like Moses, who talked with God. As it turned out, none of these ideas was exactly right because the Messiah is spiritual, not a person.

But a person, Jesus, did *show* the Jews the Messiah. He brought them a new view of the Messiah as a spiritual idea—as the understanding of their nature as God's spiritual, perfect children. Jesus not only explained this idea in words but also showed its power to heal. He proved many times that having complete faith that God is all-powerful and makes everyone spiritual—in the image and likeness of God—heals any kind of problem.

There were early signs that Jesus would introduce this new view of the Messiah, or Christ. Before Jesus' birth, Mary was told by an angel that her son would be great, that he would be called the "Son of the Highest," and that God would give him the throne of David (Luke 1:32).

Then, referring to Jesus' birth, an angel said that "a Saviour, which is Christ the Lord," had been born (Luke 2:11).

Later, when Jesus was about 30, he announced the special mission, or purpose, God had given him. While at the synagogue in Nazareth, where he grew up, he told the people that he was the one who, many years earlier, the prophet Isaiah (also known as Esaias) had promised would come to help them. The Gospel of Luke says that Jesus made this announcement by reading Isaiah's promise:

> And there was delivered unto him the book of the prophet Esaias. And when he had opened the book, he found the place where it was written, The Spirit of the Lord is upon me, because he hath anointed me to preach the gospel to the poor; he hath sent me to heal the brokenhearted, to preach deliverance to the captives, and recovering of sight to the blind, to set at liberty them that are bruised, to preach the acceptable year of the Lord. (Luke 4:17–19)

After he finished reading, Jesus made a bold statement. He told the people, "This day is this scripture fulfilled in your ears" (Luke 4:21). In other words, right there in front of them was the man Isaiah had promised would bring the good news of God's all-power and perfect love—news that would heal sickness and sin and restore life.

The Messiah and Jesus' Healing Ministry

Jesus understood that, instead of being a person, the Messiah is the Christ—his and everyone's perfect, spiritual nature, which comes from God. Instead of believing that people were sick or sinful human beings, Jesus saw their true selfhood as God's children, pure and perfect. He understood that God creates and maintains everyone's spiritual nature, and that nothing can overpower God or change what God has created. This understanding heals, as Jesus proved over and over again. At one point, when John the Baptist sent people to ask Jesus if he was the Messiah, Jesus didn't say yes and point to himself. Instead, he showed them the power of the Christ, right then and there, by healing people of all kinds of problems—blindness, sickness, lameness, and more (see Luke 7:19–22).

For three years after announcing his spiritual mission in the Nazareth synagogue, Jesus taught and healed in the cities and regions of Palestine, including Galilee, Jerusalem, Judea, and from east of the Jordan River to Decapolis, Perea, and Gaulinitis. (You can find these locations on the maps on the inside front and back covers of this book.) Most of Jesus' healings happened in Galilee, but sometimes he traveled as far away as Syria and healed people there, too.

Usually Jesus healed individuals or small groups of people. But sometimes he healed big groups of people who were diseased or paralyzed or mentally ill. No matter what was wrong, Jesus healed them. He didn't know these people's names or what they did for a living, but he knew their true nature as children of God. Jesus healed by understanding that God creates everyone spiritual and perfect—and keeps them that way.

Here's how Matthew describes Jesus healing large numbers, or multitudes, of people:

> And great multitudes came unto him,
> having with them those that were lame,
> blind, dumb, maimed, and many others,
> and cast them down at Jesus' feet; and he
> healed them: insomuch that the multi-
> tude wondered, when they saw the dumb
> to speak, the maimed to be whole, the
> lame to walk, and the blind to see: and
> they glorified the God of Israel.
> (Matthew 15:30–31)

God's Power to Heal—Available to Everyone

Jesus fulfilled the mission God had given him perfectly. But he didn't do it through his own power or ability. He knew that all power belongs to God. Once, he even said, "I can of mine own self do nothing" (John 5:30).

And another time, calling himself "Son," he said, "The Son can do nothing of himself, but what he seeth the Father do: for what things soever he doeth, these also doeth the Son likewise" (John 5:19).

Since the power to heal comes from God, Jesus knew that anyone with the same spiritual understanding he had could also heal. In fact, he taught people about their closeness to God so that everyone would be able to prove God's healing power.

Jesus definitely expected the twelve disciples who were closest to him to be healers. He told them to go out into the world and to "heal the sick, cleanse the lepers, raise the dead, cast out devils" (Matthew 10:5–8). But they weren't the only ones Jesus expected to be healers. He wanted all his followers—including those who follow his example today—to heal through the same spiritual understanding he had. Jesus said, "He that believeth on me, the works that I do shall he do also" (John 14:12).

But how could that be? Jesus had a special relationship to God. And the spiritual purpose of his life had been known and promised by Isaiah years before Jesus was born. Why would Jesus think ordinary people could heal the way he did?

The answer goes back to the Messiah, or Christ—the perfect, spiritual nature of God that was Jesus' and everyone's true selfhood. Since we are created in the image and likeness of God, divine Spirit, we are always spiritual, whole, and complete, even when it doesn't seem like it. Jesus understood that the Christ is the only truth or reality, so when he saw sickness, sin, or death, he didn't give these problems any power in his thinking. He knew these "enemies" were powerless. And the result was healing.

That is the result for anyone who understands the Christ the way Jesus did. And that's why Jesus taught others about the Christ—he wanted them to heal, too.

Sometimes Jesus taught people about the Christ through his words. Other times, he proved the power of the Christ through wonderful healings. As more and more people saw and experienced healing through the Christ, they began to realize that this spiritual understanding Jesus was bringing them must be the Messiah they had longed for.

Resistance to Jesus and His Teachings

Unfortunately, not everyone appreciated the many ways Jesus was helping and healing people. In particular, the scribes and Pharisees disliked Jesus— a lot! As they saw it, if the Jews accepted Jesus' teachings, they might think he knew more about God than the Jewish leaders did. Then people might start to ignore what the scribes and Pharisees told them to do and follow Jesus instead.

The scribes and Pharisees were so focused on the complex laws and rituals they had established that they couldn't see Jesus' healings as proof that God's power was right there with them—and with everyone. Even worse, the only way they could think of to keep their high position in Jewish society was to get rid of Jesus. In the end, though, their efforts to hurt him—and even their attempt to kill him—proved that everything Jesus had taught about God's power was true.

Jesus' life, his teachings, and his many spiritual healings show how perfectly he understood the Christ. In fact, people began using the title of "Christ" to refer to him, calling him "Christ Jesus." And just as the scribes and Pharisees had feared, more and more people started believing that the Messiah they had been waiting for was the Christ that Jesus was showing them.

The Promise of the Holy Spirit and Healing

Jesus' closest disciples understood best that he was showing them the Messiah, or Christ. And they tried to follow Jesus' example by healing through the Christ. But they still had a lot to learn. That's why they sometimes asked Jesus questions or needed his help when they couldn't heal someone.

Then, a little while before his crucifixion, Jesus told the disciples he wouldn't always be with them in person to help them. They must have been worried about how they would continue healing spiritually without him. But Jesus reassured them that they would receive the Holy Spirit (also called the "Holy Ghost") after he ascended.

The Holy Spirit is spiritual power from God. It's always with us because God is always with us, and when we turn to God in our thinking, we feel God's power and presence. Long before Jesus' time, when the great spiritual leaders and prophets in the Bible listened with all their heart to God, they felt the Holy Spirit guiding and protecting them.

Jesus brought an even higher view of the Holy Spirit. He understood the divine laws that give the Holy Spirit its power. For example, Jesus knew that God is the only power and presence and that God gives only good. Jesus also knew that God, who is Spirit, is the source of all life and keeps us safe.

And Jesus understood that we are created spiritual and perfect, in God's own image and likeness. Based on his understanding of the all-powerful, divine laws behind the Holy Spirit, Jesus knew that nothing could stop it from operating in the lives of those who love God. And knowing how much his disciples loved God, Jesus could tell them with confidence that they would receive the Holy Spirit.

When Jesus told his disciples this, he referred to the Holy Spirit as another "Comforter." He said this Comforter would always be with them to guide and help them just as he had (see John 14:16–17). This promise that they would have the Holy Spirit (also called the "Spirit of truth") right by their side must have cheered up the disciples and made them feel more confident about going forward without Jesus. They wouldn't be able to ask him questions, but their thoughts would be filled with the Holy Spirit, with the spiritual power they needed to continue Jesus' healing ministry.

Jesus' Promise Fulfilled on the Day of Pentecost

Not long after Jesus ascended, his promise about the Holy Spirit came true—not only for his closest disciples but for a big group of people. About 120 of Jesus' followers had gathered in Jerusalem to pray. Then, on the day of Pentecost, they received the Holy Spirit, just as Jesus had said they would (see Acts 1:1–8 and Acts 2:1–2, 4). This spiritual understanding and power were like a fire that couldn't be put out, and it enabled them to heal. The book of Acts says that "many wonders and signs were done by the apostles" (Acts 2:43). Here, the word "signs" means "healings." The map on the inside back cover of this book shows where many of these healings happened.

Soon, thousands of people joined Jesus' followers. They could tell by all the healings taking place that what the apostles were teaching about the Christ must be true. And they could see that these laws were true for everyone. Whoever loved the Christ and opened his or her thought to the Holy Spirit could heal. This is true today, too. Those who follow Christ Jesus—no matter who they are or where they live—can experience and share the joy of spiritual healing. The testimonies found in the "Healings from Today" section prove that. They tell about children and adults today applying spiritual laws to their problems and finding healing. The many healings in this book—during Jesus' time and today—include spiritual ideas that can help you experience healing, too.

Learn More about a Few of Jesus' Followers

Most of Jesus' followers mentioned in this book are listed in the "People" section on pages 272–278. For a few of them, you will find additional information here:

BARNABAS

Barnabas was from the island of Cyprus. He was known as a very generous man because he sold his land and donated the money to Jesus' followers in Jerusalem. He also worked faithfully to spread the gospel message—the good news about Jesus' teachings. The apostles changed his name from Joseph to "Barnabas," meaning "son of encouragement," because of his kindness, gentleness, and wonderful ability to give people hope (see Acts 4:36–37).

When the apostles in Jerusalem were afraid to accept Saul as a new follower, Barnabas spoke to them and calmed their fears (see Acts 9:26–27). Later, Barnabas was sent to Antioch to help and encourage new followers. And when the followers there needed an additional leader, Barnabas brought Saul. These two were then sent by the church to travel and share the message about Christ Jesus. When they returned to Jerusalem, they reported all the wonderful healings that had happened among the Gentiles. Later, Barnabas went on a mission with John Mark. As always, he shared the gospel message—this time on Cyprus, the island where he grew up.

JOHN

John and his older brother James were fishermen when Jesus chose them to become his disciples. John may have been the youngest of Jesus' disciples. Jesus picked John, James, and Peter to be with him at special times, such as his transfiguration and the raising of Jairus' daughter (see Matthew 17:1–8; Mark 9:2–8; Luke 9:28–36; Luke 8:40–56). Many believe John is the person referred to in the Bible as "that disciple whom Jesus loved" (John 21:7) and as the one Jesus asked to take care of his mother after he was gone. Many also believe John was the only one of Jesus' closest disciples who was at his crucifixion and the first to believe in Jesus' resurrection (see John 19:26–27; John 20:8).

After the Pentecost (see Acts 2:1–14), John and Peter healed a lame man at the Temple gate—the first recorded healing of an individual by apostles after Jesus' resurrection (see p. 180). John also taught in the Temple. He lived in Jerusalem for several years and became an important leader in the church there, but he also traveled outside Jerusalem. When Philip was successful in healing and converting Samaritans, John and Peter were sent to join him. Afterward, John and Peter preached in other places in Samaria.

PETER

Until Jesus selected them to be his disciples, Peter and his brother Andrew were fishermen. Peter was a bold, eager student. He was originally named Simon, but Jesus gave him the name Peter, which means "rock" (see Matthew 16:13–18). Jesus often chose Peter, along with James and John, to be with him at times when he wanted these disciples to have special lessons.

After Jesus was gone, Peter became a leader of the followers in Jerusalem. He was a "rock" of strength and faith, just as Jesus had said he would be. He was also a wonderful spiritual healer. Three of his healings of individuals are recorded in the Bible—two people who couldn't walk and a woman who had died (see pp. 178, 200, and 204). He also healed a group of people all at once (see Acts 5:14–16). When he was arrested for teaching about Jesus, Peter boldly continued sharing the message of God's great power and love (see Acts 5:17–29). Another time, when he was put in prison, he was freed through his prayers and those of other followers (see Acts 12:3–11). Although Peter became known as the "apostle to the Jews," he once taught a Roman centurion and his family and friends about Christ Jesus, and they became followers—the Bible says that they were filled with the Holy Spirit (see Acts 10). Peter was an enthusiastic, faithful apostle who did a great deal to bring the message of the Christ to many people.

PHILIP

The Bible tells of two men named Philip who were followers of Jesus. One was among Jesus' twelve closest disciples. The other is Philip the evangelist; this is the Philip mentioned in this book. An evangelist is one who preaches the gospel—the good news about Jesus' life and teachings. Philip the evangelist was wise and full of the Holy Spirit—the spiritual power of God. He began his mission in Jerusalem, where he was chosen to help the apostles care for the widows.

After his coworker Stephen was killed, Philip left Jerusalem to go to a city in Samaria. There he preached the good news and healed many people of illnesses, paralysis, and lameness (see p. 190).

Philip was good at listening to God's direction. Once, the thought came to him to go to a lonely desert road. He followed this divine idea, even though he didn't know why he was supposed to go there. When he arrived, he found a man from Ethiopia traveling back to his home. Philip shared the good news about Jesus with this man, and he became a follower of Christ Jesus, too (see Acts 8:26–39).

SAUL/PAUL

This apostle was from Tarsus. Although he was a Jew, he had Roman citizenship, and he spoke both Hebrew and Greek (the official language of the Roman Empire). At first, he was known by his Hebrew name, Saul, but later, when he began his missionary work, he was known by his Greek name, Paul. When he was speaking mostly to Gentiles, it probably made sense to use his Greek name since they were more likely to understand Greek than Hebrew. Also, the Bible doesn't say this, but to many Christians, the switch from using the name Saul to using Paul symbolizes his commitment to Christ.

Saul was a Pharisee. The book of Acts says he was taught by a famous teacher named Gamaliel. In his earlier life, Saul was very strict in following all the Jewish laws that Pharisees felt were important to obey. He was also a strong persecutor of Jesus' followers. Then, while on a trip to Damascus, he saw a bright light, heard a voice questioning him, and became blind. The voice said that it was Jesus speaking to him and told him to continue to Damascus and wait there. Saul was led to Damascus, and a few days after he arrived, Ananias healed him of his blindness (see p. 194). After this, Saul changed completely and had a new purpose in life. Instead of persecuting Jesus' followers, he became a follower himself and, as Paul, became perhaps the most important person in history for spreading the message of the Christ.

Filled with the Holy Spirit—spiritual power—Paul traveled with various companions by land and sea to many places in the Roman Empire. They shared the message of the Christ, gained new followers, formed new churches, and healed many people. Paul became known as the "apostle to the Gentiles" and wrote encouraging and instructive letters to several churches. Some of those letters are included in the New Testament.

Paul was often opposed by those who were jealous that people were listening to him and following him or by those who did not believe his message. At various times he was persecuted—beaten, stoned, or put in prison. But with love and joy and faith, he continued preaching the good news about Jesus' life and teachings. Paul healed himself and many other people through spiritual power alone—just as Jesus had. The Bible tells about some of these healings—of lameness, serious physical injuries, mental illness, snakebite, and stomach disease. Paul also restored a young man to life after a fall from a third-floor window. (See pp. 214–238.) Paul's life story, told in Acts, and his letters to the churches show how unselfishly and energetically he listened to and obeyed the Holy Spirit.

STEPHEN

Many people became Jesus' followers on the day of Pentecost and afterward. This increased the amount of work the apostles had to do. When they needed help distributing food to the widows, they chose seven men for this work. Stephen was one of the men chosen because he was wise, had great faith in God, and was full of the Holy Spirit. Stephen not only helped the widows but also taught and healed many people. Not everyone accepted his teaching, though. The Jewish leaders even put him on trial. What he said when he defended himself made them even angrier. A mob gathered, threw stones at Stephen, and killed him. His last words were a prayer asking God to forgive those who were stoning him: "Lord, lay not this sin to their charge" (Acts 7:60). This expression of love and forgiveness showed how faithfully Stephen followed Jesus' instruction to "love your enemies" (Matthew 5:44).

about this BOOK

Stories of Healing: Jesus and His Followers updates and consolidates a series of books published in the early 2000s. It features faithful retellings of Jesus' healing ministry recorded in the Gospels, including all 30 accounts of Jesus healing individuals or small groups of people. His healing of large groups is mentioned but not detailed here. The book also features the healing work of seven of Jesus' followers—Peter, John, Stephen, Philip, Ananias, Barnabas, and Paul—recorded in the book of Acts. Again, the healing of large groups is not presented in detail.

These retellings stay true to the biblical accounts. In those cases where more than one Gospel includes the same healing, we have typically based our retelling on the account that is richest in detail, making note in the sidebars of key differences in other accounts of the same healing. We hope bringing these stories to life in today's language helps readers of all ages get to know Jesus and his followers better and gain a clearer understanding of the spiritual truths that enabled them to heal.

A new section with contemporary testimonies of healing has been added to *Stories of Healing: Jesus and His Followers.* The testimonies written by children will be easily understood by younger readers. Others, written by adults from a more advanced perspective, may need to be explained or paraphrased for young children. This section confirms that Christian healing occurs today, just as in Jesus' time.

The Book's Organization and Approach

We have attempted to place Jesus' healings in chronological order, but none of the Gospels includes all 30 of the healings, which makes this difficult. Some of the stories are found in only one Gospel; others are found in two or three. Only two healing accounts—the restoration of Malchus' ear and Jesus' resurrection—are found in all four Gospels. As a result, no exact chronology is known, but we have ordered the stories according to Bible scholars' best understanding. The healings by Jesus' followers are arranged as they appear in the book of Acts.

Additional information about Bible times, people, and customs has been added to make the stories more understandable. These additions are supported by Bible scholarship in the sources listed in the bibliography (p. 294). The inside of the front and back covers of the book feature maps showing the places where Jesus' healings and those of his followers took place.

To help readers gain a deeper understanding of these healing accounts, the spiritual truths that enabled Jesus and his followers to heal are explained according to Christian Science. These truths are based on the Bible and *Science and Health with Key to the Scriptures* by Mary Baker Eddy, the Discoverer and Founder of Christian Science. Among these fundamental spiritual truths are Jesus' understanding of God, divine Spirit, as all-powerful and entirely good; his recognition of God as the sole creator and of God's creation as spiritual and perfect; and his view of everyone's true nature as the pure and perfect child of God. On the basis of these truths, Jesus and his followers could see beyond the material picture of a sick or sinful person to the individual's spiritual selfhood, created and maintained by God. This realization of God's all-powerful goodness in operation right where the problem appeared to be brought healing.

Ways to Read This Book

As explained on p. 10, each account in this book includes additional information in the sidebars and also directs the reader—through color coding—to sections in the back of the book with entries on the people, places, customs, terms, and concepts relevant to the story. The sidebars and back sections will be of interest to older children and adult readers. But they are not essential to understanding what happens in the stories. In fact, we recommend at least once reading the book from beginning to end without stopping to digest the related information in the sidebars and back sections. This type of straightforward read-through provides an overarching and inspiring view of the extensive healing work Jesus and his followers accomplished.

In addition, this book is a reference tool for diving into particular stories, reviewing the healing work of specific disciples, or focusing on healings of certain problems, such as paralysis or blindness. In these cases, the sidebars and relevant entries in the back sections will be helpful. We hope the background material and explanation of spiritual concepts in "The Life and Times of Jesus" will be useful as well. Some of this information may be familiar, but we believe most readers will find new insights in these pages.

The language in the stories will likely be accessible to children in early elementary school, but the sidebars and reference sections in the back may be beyond their reading level and comprehension. In that case, we recommend having an older child or adult guide them through this material, singling out the most important points and putting them into words they can understand. Very young children may need help understanding some of the stories. In those cases, having someone older paraphrase them and possibly skip the more complicated parts will be helpful. That individual may also want to discuss which aspects of the story are depicted in the illustrations, since this often helps younger readers grasp and retain the story's key elements.

We hope children and adults alike enjoy working with this book and find frequent opportunities to read one or more healing accounts together. These accounts offer a wonderful springboard for discussing the proofs of God's goodness people are experiencing today and the ways we can all follow Jesus' example.

BIBLIOGRAPHY

General

Arlandson, James Malcolm. *Women, Class, and Society in Early Christianity.* Peabody, MA: Hendrickson, 1997.

Brown, Raymond E. *An Introduction to the New Testament.* New York: Doubleday, 1997.

Buckmaster, Henrietta. *Paul: A Man who Changed the World.* New York: McGraw-Hill, 1965.

Conybeare, The Rev. W. J., and The Very Rev. J. S. Howson. *The Life and Epistles of St. Paul.* Grand Rapids, MI: W. B. Eerdmans, 1954.

Deen, Edith. *All of the Women of the Bible.* San Francisco: Harper & Row, 1955.

Eddy, Mary Baker. *Prose Works Other than "Science and Health with Key to the Scriptures."* Boston: The First Church of Christ, Scientist, 1953.

Eddy, Mary Baker. *Science and Health with Key to the Scriptures.* Boston: The First Church of Christ, Scientist, 1934.

Goodspeed, Edgar J. *Paul.* Philadelphia: John C. Winston, 1947.

Graser, Audrey. *Morning Glory: The Story of the First Christians and Their Risen Christ.* Lincolnshire, England: Autumn House, 2000.

Harris, Stephen L. *The New Testament: A Student's Introduction.* Mountain View, CA: Mayfield, 1995.

Kee, Howard Clark, Franklin W. Young, and Karlfried Froehlich. *Understanding the New Testament.* Englewood Cliffs, NJ: Prentice-Hall, 1965.

Maier, Paul L. *In the Fullness of Time.* San Francisco: Harper & Row, 1991.

Meinardus, Otto F. A. *St. Paul in Greece.* Athens: Lycabettus Press, 1977.

Miller, Rex. *I, Paul.* Granada Hills, CA: The Friendly Shop, 1988.

Robinson, Russell D. *Teaching the Scriptures.* Milwaukee: Bible Study, 1993.

Sergio, Lisa. *Jesus and Woman.* McLean, VA: EPM Publications, 1975.

Severy, Merle, ed. *Greece and Rome: Builders of Our World.* Washington, DC: National Geographic Society, 1968.

Shepard, J. W. *The Life and Letters of St. Paul.* Grand Rapids, MI: W. B. Eerdmans, 1950.

Trench, Richard C. *Notes on the Miracles of Our Lord.* Grand Rapids, MI: Baker, 1949.

Trueblood, Elton. *The Humor of Christ.* San Francisco: Harper & Row, 1964.

Bibles

The Amplified Bible. Grand Rapids, MI: Zondervan, 1965.

Costecalde, Claude-Bernard, ed. *The Illustrated Family Bible.* New York: DK, 1997.

Gaus, Andy. *The Unvarnished New Testament.* Grand Rapids, MI: Phanes, 1991.

Good News Bible: Today's English Version. Nashville: Thomas Nelson, 1976.

Hastings, Selina. *The Children's Illustrated Bible.* New York: DK, 1994.

The Holy Bible: Authorized King James Version.

The Living Bible. Wheaton, IL: Tyndale, 1976.

New International Version. Wheaton, IL: Tyndale, 1984.

The New Jerusalem Bible. New York: Doubleday, 1990.

New Living Translation. Wheaton, IL: Tyndale, 1996.

Peterson, Eugene H. *The Message.* Colorado Springs: NavPress, 1995.

Phillips, J. B. *The New Testament in Modern English.* New York: Macmillan, 1972.

Dictionaries and Concordances

Butler, Trent C., ed. *Holman Bible Dictionary.* Nashville: B&H Publishing, 1991.

Buttrick, George Arthur, ed. *The Interpreter's Dictionary of the Bible.* Nashville: Abingdon, 1962.

Freedman, David Noel, ed. *The Anchor Bible Dictionary.* New York: Doubleday, 1992.

Hastings, James, ed. *Dictionary of the Bible.* New York: Charles Scribner's Sons, 1963.

Illustrated Dictionary of Bible Life and Times. Pleasantville, NY: Reader's Digest, 1997.

Neusner, Jacob, ed. *Dictionary of Judaism in the Biblical Period.* Peabody, MA: Hendrickson, 1966.

Orr, James, ed. *International Standard Bible Encyclopedia.* Chicago: The Howard-Severance Company, 1915.

Powell, Mark Allan, ed. *HarperCollins Bible Dictionary.* New York: HarperCollins, 2011.

Smith, Barbara. *Young People's Bible Dictionary.* Philadelphia: Westminster, 1965.

Strong, James. *The Exhaustive Concordance of the Bible.* Nashville: Abingdon, 1980.

Thayer, Joseph H. *Thayer's Greek-English Lexicon of the New Testament.* Grand Rapids, MI: Baker, 1977.

Commentaries

Barclay, William. *The Daily Study Bible.* Philadelphia: Westminster, 1975.

Buttrick, George Arthur, ed. *The Interpreter's Bible.* Nashville: Abigdon, 1982.

Dummelow, Rev. J. R., ed. *A Commentary on the Holy Bible.* New York: Macmillan, 1939.

Gaebelein, Frank E., ed. *The Expositor's Bible Commentary.* Grand Rapids, MI: Zondervan, 1984.

Harrison, Everett G., ed. *The Wycliffe Bible Commentary.* Nashville: Southwestern, 1962.

Henry, Matthew. *Commentary on the Whole Bible.* Edited by Rev. Leslie F. Church. Grand Rapids, MI: Zondervan, 1961.

Jamieson, Robert, A. E. Fausset, and David Brown, eds. *Jamieson, Fausset & Brown's Commentary on the Whole Bible.* Grand Rapids, MI: Zondervan, 1961.

Keck, Leander E., ed. *The New Interpreter's Bible.* Nashville: Abingdon, 1995.

Laymon, Charles M., ed. *The Interpreter's One-Volume Commentary on the Bible.* Nashville: Abingdon, 1971.

Mays, James L., ed. *Harper's Bible Commentary.* San Francisco: Harper & Row, 1988.

Morris, Canon Leon, ed. *The Tyndale New Testament Commentaries.* Grand Rapids, MI: W. B. Eerdmans, 1985.

Stern, David S. *Jewish New Testament Commentary.* Clarksville, MD: Jewish New Testament Publications, 1995.

Williams, David J. *New International Biblical Commentary.* Peabody, MA: Hendrickson, 1990.

Atlases

Frank, Harry Thomas, ed. *Atlas of the Bible Lands.*
Maplewood, NJ: Hammond, 1990.

May, Herbert G., ed. *Oxford Bible Atlas.* Oxford:
Oxford University Press, 1976.

Wright, George Ernest, and Floyd Vivian Filson,
eds. *The Westminster Historical Atlas of the Bible.*
Philadelphia: Westminster, 1946.

Daily Life in Bible Times

Connolly, Peter. *Living in the Time of Jesus of
Nazareth.* Oxford: Oxford University Press, 1983.

Derrett, J. Duncan M. *Jesus's Audience.* New York:
Seabury, 1973.

Gower, Ralph. *The New Manners and Customs of Bible
Times.* Chicago: Moody, 1987.

Miller, J. Lane, and Madeleine S. Miller. *Harper's
Encyclopedia of Bible Life.* Edison, NJ: Castle, 1978.

Thompson, J. A. *Handbook of Life in Bible Times.*
Madison, WI: Inter-Varsity, 1986.

INDEX

Page numbers in **bold** indicate primary entries
found in the definitions sections on pages 261–282.

about the
AUTHORS

MARY JO BEEBE is a freelance writer and editor whose interest in Bible research was inspired by trips to Israel, Greece, and Turkey. A longtime Sunday School teacher, with a degree in English from the University of North Texas, she has decades of experience writing and editing children's activity books, training programs, business books, and marketing materials.

OLENE CARROLL is a writer, Bible researcher, and speaker. For several years her Bible scholarship resulted in a weekly research newsletter. With Nancy Fischer, she co-hosted Bible tours to the Holy Land, Greece, Egypt, and Turkey. In 1997 she participated in the archaeological dig at Bethsaida, on the northern shore of the Sea of Galilee. She graduated from Florida State University with a degree in Elementary Education.

NANCY FISCHER was a writer, Bible researcher, and speaker. With Olene Carroll, she led numerous tours of the Holy Land, Greece, Egypt, and Turkey. Nancy participated in the 1997 archaeological dig at Bethsaida. A former high school English teacher, she taught Sunday School for over 30 years. She graduated from Coe College with a double major in English and Music.

about the
ILLUSTRATOR

GENEVIEVE MEEK is an award-winning illustrator whose contemporary designs have appeared in many places, including children's books, such as the Wishbone mystery books. She holds a degree in Communication and Arts from Southern Methodist University.

Rome

ITALY

ILLYRICUM

MACEDONIA

Philippi

Thessalonica

Mysia

Troas

Aegean Sea

Corinth

Athens

Ephesus

ACHAIA
(Greece)

MELITA

MAP 2
Places where Jesus and
his early followers healed

● Locations of healings
● Other places mentioned in this book

0   50   100   150   200 miles

0   100   200   300 km